PRACTICE MAKES PERFECT

Preparation for
State Reading
Assessments

LEVEL **7**

PRESTWICK HOUSE
INCORPORATED

P.O. Box 658 • Clayton, Delaware 19938

AUTHOR: Sondra Y. Abel

EDITOR: Mary C. Beardsley

REVIEWING TEACHERS: Barbara Bretherick, Wellington, FL
Catherine O. Routh, Helena, GA

COVER DESIGN: Larry Knox

PRODUCTION: Jerry Clark

PRESTWICK HOUSE, INC.
P.O. BOX 658 • CLAYTON, DELAWARE 19938
TEL: 1.800.932.4593
FAX: 1.888.718.9333
WEB: www.prestwickhouse.com

ISBN 978-1-58049-316-1

Preparation for
State Reading Assessments

Table of Contents

How to Take a Reading Comprehension Test

Taking a reading comprehension test does not have to be a stressful event. The following tips and methods can be used to make your test-taking efforts more effective and your results more accurate.

FOCUS:

When you read a comprehension passage, you should try to identify the following:

- main idea ● author's attitude or tone ● author's purpose

Many comprehension questions focus on your ability to determine what the author is trying to say and why he or she is saying it. Think about whether the author is biased: does he or she support, criticize, or remain objective about the subject? What clues show the author's attitude?

While you read, you should imagine yourself as the test writer.

- Which pieces of information do you think are important?
- Is the passage about a person or a group of people?
- What is that person's or group's message to the world?
- What questions would you write about the passage?

When you come across a point that stands out, make a mental note of it. Ask yourself why the author included it. Information that seems to have a special purpose often shows up in the questions.

TIPS:

In order to determine an author's attitude toward the subject, look for emotionally charged words, such as *tragically, sadly, unfortunately, surprisingly, amazingly, justly,* etc. These words indicate an author's bias—whether the author sides with or against the subject of the passage. Simple words tell you a lot about the author's feelings.

Frequently, you are asked to identify the main idea of a passage. These types of questions do not always use the words *main idea*. They may ask for the most appropriate title or the statement with which the author would most likely agree or disagree. Pick the answer that is true for the entire passage. If no choice relates to the entire selection, choose the answer that is supported by most of the passage.

You will also encounter questions that ask you to define a word or find the most appropriate synonym. These questions check your ability to use context clues, not your vocabulary knowledge. Sometimes, you will find more than one seemingly correct answer, but when you look at the word as it is used in the paragraph, you can choose the best synonym for the situation.

Some questions are open-ended and require you to write an answer. You must write two-to-four complete sentences to answer these types of questions. The person who scores your answer will look for you to explain yourself, so be sure to support your opinion with details from the passage.

Finally, when it comes to taking timed tests, many people feel pressured to race through the work so that they complete all of it. Remember, though, that careful reading cannot be rushed. So, what can you do? When you cannot decide the answer to a question, skip it and come back to it after you have answered the rest of the questions for that passage. You may even find the answer when you are working on other questions. If you still cannot answer it, make your best guess and move on, rather than spend too much time trying to figure out one question, leaving yourself insufficient time to answer the rest accurately.

Some people suggest reading the questions before you read the passage so that you know what information you need. If this works for you, that is terrific! For many people, however, this uses valuable time and results in too much information to remember. This breaks their concentration, and they cannot focus on what they read. If you cannot focus on both the questions and the reading at one time, read the passage first, concentrating on what you read. If you need to look back at the passage to answer the questions, go ahead and do so. The point to be made here is that you should work in a manner that is comfortable for you. When you find a technique that works for you, use it!

REMEMBER THESE THREE EXTREMELY IMPORTANT POINTS:

1. **Read the directions and questions carefully!**
   Look for tricky words, such as *not, always, true, opposite,* etc. These words greatly affect the answer to the question.

2. **If you cannot remember what you just read, read it again, and pay attention to it!**

3. **Always read all the answer choices!**
   You may choose the wrong answer and miss the correct one entirely if you stop reading once you think you have found the answer. There may be a better choice farther down the list, and you will miss it if you do not read it.

Model Passage

The following model passage demonstrates effective use of the reading tips and strategies. You will see that there are underlined words and phrases in the passage and notes in the margins. The notes in the margins refer to the underlined portions of the passage and serve as examples of the way you should think about the passage. These notes include questions you should ask yourself or comments you should make to yourself as you read.

The Railroads Connect

[1]This passage will be about the disorder of the "Wedding of the Rails" celebration.

On May 10, 1869, the Transcontinental Railroad was finally connected after years of hard work and confusion, but the celebration of the "Wedding of the Rails" was plagued by disorder and misunderstanding.[1]

[2]What are the funny errors?

[3]The points are organized. The word *first* tells me to look for *second*, etc. Look for *next* and *finally*.

[4]Wow, that is only six days before the ceremony.

[5]Wow, $400 of his own gold! Why? What kind of question will the test ask about this?

[6]I should look at the context of these boldfaced words. What do they mean?

[7]Those spikes were just dropped in the holes!

[8]This was a huge event if the telegraph was going to relay the sound.

Of course, the real story is a comedy of errors.[2] First[3] the actual location of the event was Promontory Summit, Utah, but since this was not on the map, the press reported that it occurred at Promontory Point; therefore, postcards, souvenirs, and even textbooks to this day bear the name of the incorrect location. Second, on May 4, 1869,[4] the president of the Central Pacific Railroad, Leland Stanford, revealed to his friend, David Hewes, that no commemorative item had been made for the event. Upset by this fact, Hewes attempted to have a solid gold rail made, but after failing to find someone to finance it, he had $400 worth of his own gold melted and cast[5] as the "Golden Spike," which was then engraved[6] for the occasion. Three other spikes were also made for the event. The next problem arose when the event had to be postponed because disgruntled[6] workers and poor weather conditions delayed the arrival of officials from the Union Pacific Railroad. Finally, on May 10, 1869, the officials from both the Union Pacific and the Central Pacific railroads convened for the celebration. A special laurelwood railroad tie was laid in place at the junction, and the specially-made spikes were dropped into pre-drilled holes. Not one of them was actually hammered into place.[7] Then, the laurelwood tie and spikes were replaced with a standard tie and regular iron spikes. The last spike and the hammer were connected to the telegraph line so that the entire nation could hear[8] the "Wedding of the

⁹The name of the event is mentioned again. This must be important.

¹⁰That is funny—after all of the problems, the important people who were supposed to hammer the spike could not do it.

¹¹That is funny, too. I cannot believe no one showed up. It seems as if no one cared.

Rails."⁹ The sound of the hammer hitting the spike would then travel across the country through the telegraph line. Leland Stanford was given the first swing, but he missed¹⁰ the spike and hit the wooden tie. Thomas Durant, vice president of the Union Pacific Railroad, swung at the spike, but missed entirely. In the end, a railroad employee hammered in the final tie,¹⁰ and the telegraph operator sent the message to the country: "D-O-N-E."

Not so surprisingly, when the fiftieth anniversary celebration was scheduled, not one person showed up.¹¹ Maybe they all went to Promontory Point.

1. Which of the following best states the author's purpose?

    A. to make fun of the Transcontinental Railroad

    B. to make an accurate portrayal of an important event in railroad history

    C. to explain the importance of the Golden Spike

    D. to describe how history books sometimes contain incorrect information

(B) The author accurately describes the confusion and mishaps surrounding the "Wedding of the Rails" celebration. All other answer choices are merely supporting points in the passage.

2. Which of the following would be the best title for this passage?

    A. The Golden Spike Disaster

    B. Where the Railroads Meet

    C. Leland Stanford's Spike

    D. The Wedding of the Rails

(D) The passage is about the entire "Wedding of the Rails" ceremony. After all, the ceremony's title is mentioned twice in the passage, making it significant information appropriate for the title. Although the event was riddled with errors, it would not be considered a disaster. Finally, the passage does not focus solely on Leland Stanford's spike or where the event occurred.

3. Which of the following did not lend to the confusion on May 10, 1869?

    A. the telegraph operator

    B. poor weather conditions

    C. last-minute planning

    D. uncertainty about the location

(A) *The telegraph operator does not make any errors. The poor weather postponed officials; last minute planning required a friend to donate his own gold for the commemorative spike; uncertainty about the location led to incorrect information.*

4. As used in the passage, the word *engraved* most nearly means

    A. molded.

    B. decorated.

    C. transported.

    D. purchased.

(B) *If the spike was <u>engraved</u> for the occasion, it must have been decorated to show its commemorative purpose. <u>Molded</u> is not the answer because the passage already stated that the gold was melted and cast. Although the spike would have to be <u>transported</u>, the context is discussing the making of the spike, not the shipping of the spike. Finally, the gold was already <u>purchased</u> since it belonged to Hewes.*

5. Based on the information provided in the passage, what can you infer is the reason for David Hewes's melting his own gold to make the spike?

    A. He was angry that no one would help him.

    B. He wanted to become famous for his contribution to the Transcontinental Railroad.

    C. He could find no one willing to pay for or donate the gold.

    D. He had more gold than he needed, so he was willing to give some away.

(C) *Hewes tried to find someone to finance a rail but was unsuccessful. Had he found someone willing to pay or donate at least something, then he would not have had to use his own resources. Since he looked for someone to finance a golden rail instead of financing it himself, we can infer that he did not have an overabundance of gold. There are no clues to imply he was searching for fame. Finally, the passage states that he was upset that there was no item made to commemorate the event, but makes no mention of his being angry at finding no one willing to help.*

6. *Answer the following question using complete sentences:*
   Why does the author call the "Wedding of the Rails" a "comedy of errors"?

The event is humorous because it was a major celebration of the uniting of the country's rails, which was a massive undertaking, and everything that could go wrong did. Railroad officials arrived late because their workers were unhappy, the commemorative spike was not even hammered in, and a railroad employee, not any of the officials who organized the celebration, completed the actual connection of the rails. As a final taunt, no one showed up for the fiftieth anniversary celebration.

DIRECTIONS: *Read the passage and answer the questions that follow it.*

Nobel's Intentions

WINNING THE NOBEL PRIZE is one of the greatest honors a person can earn for his or her work. Alfred Nobel established the Nobel Prize in 1895, through a fund in his will. Nobel was a Swedish chemist who invented dynamite for its beneficial purposes. When he saw people using dynamite for war, he was deeply saddened. He then decided to use his fortune to reward people who worked for peace and the good of mankind.

Individuals and organizations receive nominations for this award based on their contributions to society. Awards are presented in each of the following fields: economics, physics, chemistry, physiology or medicine, peace, and literature. Every year, between 100 and 250 nominees are chosen for each prize. Any living person, of any nationality, can be nominated for the Nobel Prize. However, only people within certain organizations are allowed to make nominations, and individuals may not nominate themselves. The Nobel institutions do not announce nominees, and then, the nominee records are sealed for fifty years.

Since 1901, 776 Nobel Prizes have been awarded. The award may be shared by up to three people or given to an organization. Some famous Nobel Prize winners include: President Theodore Roosevelt (1906), Martin Luther King, Jr. (1964), and Mother Teresa of Calcutta (1979).

The Nobel Prize award ceremony is held in the Stockholm Concert Hall in Sweden and the Oslo City Hall in Norway. The ceremonies take place every year on the anniversary of Alfred Nobel's death: December 10th. Those who win the prize receive a gold medal, a diploma, and money. Today, the prize money amounts to approximately 1.3 million U.S. dollars per award. With this amount of money, many winners retire (if they have not done so already) or make donations to good causes. However, Alfred Nobel **intended** the money to be used as funding, so the winner could continue his or her work and research for the benefit of society.

QUESTIONS

1. Which one of the following statements is true?
   A. Anyone can make a nomination for a Nobel Prize.
   B. The award ceremony is held in the Stockholm Concert Hall in Sweden.
   C. Alfred Nobel invented dynamite to help his country win a war.
   D. Any living person can be nominated for a Nobel Prize.

2. Which of the following best states the author's purpose?
   A. to show how people who work to benefit society are never recognized
   B. to explain the significance of the Nobel Prize
   C. to show how the Nobel Prize is only awarded to famous people
   D. to show how people's intentions are never followed

3. As used in the passage, the word *intended* most nearly means
   A. designed.
   B. followed.
   C. forced.
   D. invented.

4. Which of the following statements best describes the reason for the last paragraph?
   A. It tells when Alfred Nobel died.
   B. It mentions some famous Nobel Prize winners.
   C. It gives the details of the ceremony and the award.
   D. It defines the word *intended*.

5. Which statement best describes the creation of the Nobel Prize?
   A. The Nobel Prize was created by famous people who wanted to recognize others in their fields of study.
   B. The Nobel Prize was created to recognize people who help society.
   C. The Nobel Prize was created to bring more people into the fields of science and technology.
   D. The Nobel Prize was created to show how good inventions could be used for the wrong purposes.

6. *Answer the following question using complete sentences:*
   Why might the nominee records of the Nobel Prize be sealed for fifty years?

DIRECTIONS: *Read the passage and answer the questions that follow it.*

The Marathon

IN ANCIENT TIMES, Greece was a war-riddled territory. The people of Athens, Greece, frequently fought others who threatened their customs and ways of life. In 490 BC, they battled the Persians in the city of Marathon, Greece. The Persians were fierce fighters and had more soldiers than the Athenians. The soldiers of Athens were worried that they would lose this important battle. Surprisingly, the Athenian soldiers won. According to legend, a messenger named Pheidippides ran nearly twenty-five miles from Marathon to Athens to give the news about the victory. When he got to Athens, he shouted "Niki!" which means victory, then collapsed and died from exhaustion. The modern Athens marathon was born to **commemorate** Pheidippides' journey from the battlefield.

In 1896, Pheidippides' legendary feat was repeated when the Greeks hosted their first Olympic games. They created a 24.86-mile run from Marathon Bridge to the Olympic stadium in Athens. A Greek runner, Spiridon Louis, won the race with a time of two hours, fifty-eight minutes, and fifty seconds. Since then, Athens has held an annual marathon that attracts people from all over the globe. The marathon's one-hundredth anniversary in 1996 attracted 3,000 runners.

The marathon is still run in the Olympic games today, but the distance has changed. In 1908, the Olympic games were held in London, England. Here, the runners were to travel from Windsor Castle to White Clay Stadium. The extra distance of almost two miles was added so the race would finish in front of the royal family's viewing box at the stadium. Although the English may cry out "God save the Queen!" at the twenty-four-mile mark, Pheidippides' cry of victory can be heard by all those who cross the finish line—no matter what country they call home. ●

QUESTIONS

1. **Which of the following would be the best title for this passage?**
   - **A.** Pheidippides
   - **B.** Birth of the Marathon
   - **C.** Greek Legends
   - **D.** The Olympic Games

2. **Which of the following best states the author's purpose?**
   - **A.** to show how government rulers impact sports
   - **B.** to show how many people participate in marathons
   - **C.** to show how fierce Greeks were in battle
   - **D.** to explain how the marathon was born

3. **Which of the following statements best describes the reason for the first paragraph?**
   - **A.** to show how legends are never true
   - **B.** to define *commemorate*
   - **C.** to describe who Pheidippides was
   - **D.** to give a lesson about Greek geography

4. **Which of the following best describes the reason for Pheidippides' run?**
   - **A.** He was training for the Olympic games.
   - **B.** He was giving news about a battle victory.
   - **C.** He was fleeing from the battle against the Persians.
   - **D.** He was going to see the Queen of England.

5. **As used in the passage, the word *commemorate* most nearly means to**
   - **A.** memorialize.
   - **B.** forget.
   - **C.** watch.
   - **D.** prove.

6. **Which of the following statements best describes the reason for the last paragraph?**
   - **A.** It describes how the marathon was born.
   - **B.** It explains the origin of the saying "God save the Queen!"
   - **C.** It shows how sports can change with time, location, and political influence.
   - **D.** It shows how the marathon is only performed in Greece.

DIRECTIONS: *Read the passage and answer the questions that follow it.*

Plants

WHILE IT IS NOT UNCOMMON to see an insect eating a plant, sometimes the reverse is true, quite possibly more often than you think. There are several types of insect-eating plants that live in the United States. These plants often inhabit the wet soils of marshes and bogs. These soils lack nitrogen, which is an essential nutrient for plant growth. These plants **derive** nitrogen from insects after trapping and digesting them.

The most popular insect-eating plant is perhaps the Venus flytrap. The leaves of the flytrap are clam-shaped with spikes around the edges. When an insect lands on the flytrap, the leaves snap shut, and the spikes trap the insect inside. Although it is called a flytrap, the plant mostly eats crawling insects because it is more difficult for them to escape. The largest insect-eating plant is the pitcher plant. This plant gets its name from the leaves, shaped like pitchers, which collect rainwater. The rim of the pitcher has stiff, downward pointing hairs. When insects enter the "pitcher," the hairs trap the insects, which are now unable to escape. The insects then fall into the bottom of the pitcher, drown, and are digested. The sundew plant consumes insects with its acid. The leaves of the plant use sticky tentacles to trap an insect for a meal. The bladderwort traps insects similarly to the Venus flytrap. The bladderwort is a water plant that has many small bladders, which have trapdoors and sensitive bristles. When an insect touches a bristle, the trapdoor pulls water and the insect inside the bladder before digesting it. Although these plants have an unorthodox method of gathering nutrients, they are truly fascinating specimens. ❂

QUESTIONS

1. Which of the following would be the best title for this passage?
   A. Dangerous Plants
   B. Insect Eaters
   C. Water Plants
   D. Eating Insects

2. Which of the following best states the author's purpose?
   A. to show how plants get their nutrients
   B. to show that insect-eating plants are mythic creatures
   C. to explain how different insect-eating plants function
   D. to explain why plants eat insects

3. As used in the passage, the word *derive* most nearly means
   A. obtain.
   B. strangle.
   C. create.
   D. swallow.

4. According to the passage, why do these plants eat insects?
   A. The plants eat insects because there are no other nutrients for them.
   B. The plants eat insects because the soil does not have enough nutrients.
   C. The plants eat insects because they live in water and do not have access to soil.
   D. The plants eat insects only when other animals are unavailable.

5. What is the difference between the bladderwort and the Venus flytrap?
   A. The bladderwort does not trap insects like the Venus flytrap.
   B. The bladderwort eats flying insects, and the Venus flytrap eats insects that live in the soil.
   C. The bladderwort uses acid to digest insects but the flytrap does not.
   D. The bladderwort is a water plant while the flytrap lives in soil.

6. Which statement is true?
   A. The Venus flytrap is the most popular insect-eating plant.
   B. The pitcher plant uses acid to digest insects.
   C. The sundew plant lives in water.
   D. The bladderwort plant is the largest insect-eating plant.

DIRECTIONS: *Read the passage and answer the questions that follow it.*

Crazy Horse,
a Man of Principle

CRAZY HORSE, KNOWN for his leadership and bravery, was a famous Native American war chief of the Sioux tribe. Born around 1840 in South Dakota, he was given his name by his father, a medicine man, after proving his skill and bravery in combat.

During the 1800s, the U.S. Army **conducted** military operations to drive the Native Americans off the land and onto reservations. Crazy Horse firmly believed that the settlers were a threat to the Native Americans' way of life, and in his early twenties, he began combating U.S. soldiers in an effort to preserve Native American culture. During many battles, Crazy Horse acted as a decoy to draw soldiers away from their defenses. Crazy Horse joined with Sitting Bull in the late 1870s to defend their land in the Black Hills. The Army had a three-pronged plan to defeat the Sioux. Crazy Horse and his men confronted the troops led by Gen. George Crook at Rosebud Creek on June 17, 1876, and emerged victorious. After this battle, the Sioux rode to Little Bighorn and joined forces with Sitting Bull's men. Eight days later, Gen. George Custer and his men attacked the camp. Although Crazy Horse and Sitting Bull were victorious in this battle also, the military continued to fight for the land.

With the continuing wars, Sitting Bull fled to Canada. Crazy Horse tried to hold areas of Yellowstone but also grew tired of fighting. He decided to move to the reservation he was promised and turned himself in on May 6, 1877, near Fort Robinson. While he spent the summer waiting to be transferred to the reservation, many rumors about him spread. Because one rumor claimed that Crazy Horse was planning to escape, he was arrested on the fifth of September. Realizing that the captors were also going to lock him into a guardhouse, Crazy Horse struggled against them, but was tragically stabbed to death.

Crazy Horse was a great hero who fought bravely out of loyalty to his people and love of his culture. His spirit is honored in the Black Hills of South Dakota at the Crazy Horse Memorial, a grand sculpture that has been under construction for well over half a century.

QUESTIONS

1. Which of the following best states the author's purpose?

  A. to describe the life of a famous Indian war chief

  B. to describe the battles over America's land

  C. to compare the leadership styles of Crazy Horse and Sitting Bull

  D. to show how the settlers ruined the lives of the Indians

2. With which of the following statements would Crazy Horse most likely agree?

  A. The settlers had as much right to the land as the Sioux.

  B. The settlers threatened the Sioux's culture.

  C. Crazy Horse fought because he wanted people to know who he was.

  D. Crazy Horse fought because he hoped to get rid of the settlers.

3. As used in the passage, the word *conducted* most nearly means

  A. battled.

  B. followed.

  C. planned.

  D. engaged.

4. Which of the following statements best describes the reason for the second paragraph?

  A. It informs the reader about Gen. Custer's famous battle.

  B. It describes how Crazy Horse became a famous warrior.

  C. It describes how Crazy Horse died.

  D. It describes the U.S. Army's actions against all the Indians.

5. According to the passage, how did Crazy Horse die?

  A. Crazy Horse was murdered when he tried to escape from being locked up.

  B. Crazy Horse died fighting beside his men in battle.

  C. Crazy Horse died while being transported to a reservation.

  D. Crazy Horse died after his own men stabbed him.

6. According to the passage, why did so many battles occur between the U.S. Army and the Sioux?

  A. The Sioux did not want to move to Canada.

  B. The Army was a prejudiced group that hated the Sioux.

  C. The government wanted the Sioux's land.

  D. The Sioux did not want to share the land.

DIRECTIONS: *Read the passage and answer the questions that follow it.*

Knighthood

MEDIEVAL EUROPE WAS a turbulent place, dominated by disputes and battles over land, nobility, and honor. Soldiers on horseback fought with swords and wore protective armor and helmets. These warriors, called "knights," owned land and pledged loyalty to a "lord" (a king, prince, or nobleman). Those to whom they pledged their loyalty would offer land and protection as long as these knights served in military duty against the enemies.

As landowners, these knights could not go away for extended periods of military duty since they had to take care of their land and families. Regardless, a nobleman needed soldiers to fight long wars. Because of these situations, a landowner's son could fight in his father's place. First, the son had to prove that he could use a sword and ride horseback. To practice these skills, young men participated in **tournaments** in which they fought against each other. After proving his skill, a young man would kneel in front of his nobleman. The nobleman would touch the man on the shoulder with his sword and say, "I dub thee Sir… [whatever the man's name was]." By this, a young man would become a knight.

Later, a more complicated system for knighthood developed. At age seven or eight, a free landowner's son would leave his family to become a page. A page lived in a nobleman's castle to learn how knights became brave warriors. When the boy became a teenager, he would become a squire. A squire was a knight's servant; he helped prepare a knight for battle by riding with him and carrying his equipment. If a squire was brave and faithful, he would be knighted.

When a man was knighted, he agreed to follow certain rules, called codes of chivalry. These codes included being courteous and helpful to women. During times of war, such as the Holy Crusades, knights made vows of poverty and obedience. Since fighting styles and military needs have changed greatly, knighthood is now reserved as an honor granted in recognition of great accomplishments. ◉

QUESTIONS

1. **Which quality would a successful medieval knight possess?**
   - **A.** dishonesty
   - **B.** bravery
   - **C.** weaponry
   - **D.** land

2. **Which of the following best states the author's purpose?**
   - **A.** to show how knighthood was important during the medieval period
   - **B.** to show how noblemen fought their wars
   - **C.** to explain how a man became a knight
   - **D.** to explain why the chivalry code was invented

3. **As used in the passage, the word *tournaments* most nearly means**
   - **A.** contests.
   - **B.** festivals.
   - **C.** parades.
   - **D.** wars.

4. **Which of the following statements best describes the reason for the second paragraph?**
   - **A.** It shows the importance of tournaments to knights in training.
   - **B.** It shows how noblesman's sons were first chosen to be knights.
   - **C.** It shows how the oldest son was sacrificed for battle.
   - **D.** It explains why so many men died in wars.

5. **According to the third paragraph, how did a man become a knight?**
   - **A.** A man was dubbed a knight after becoming a page.
   - **B.** A boy would work for a nobleman and after many years was dubbed a knight.
   - **C.** A boy would go through different stages and learn about knighthood.
   - **D.** The youngest son was sent with a nobleman who taught him how to fight in battle.

6. **How did knights fight during medieval times?**
   - **A.** Knights fought in tournaments against one another.
   - **B.** Knights fought only in holy wars.
   - **C.** Knights fought against landowners, peasants, and kings.
   - **D.** Knights fought on horseback for their lords.

DIRECTIONS: *Read the passage and answer the questions that follow it.*

Bats

FOR CENTURIES, MYTHS and fantastic stories have led to an unfounded fear of bats. In reality, however, bats pose very little threat to humans and, in some cases, are even beneficial. Perhaps the greatest bat myth of all centers on vampire bats, which are not vampires at all—they do not morph from human to bat form, nor do they swoop in through bedroom windows to feast on human blood. Natives of South America, vampire bats feed on the blood of birds and other animals. In order for one of these bats to attack a human, all of its other food sources would have to be depleted. Most bats, though, procure their **sustenance** from insects and the nectar from flowers. The entire ecosystem benefits from these bats because they help control the insect population. For example, one bat can eat thousands of mosquitoes, thinning out the numbers of these pests. Bats that eat nectar cross-pollinate plants that we use for medicines, bandages, and food. Without the bats' help, these plants would not be able to reproduce.

Have you ever seen a bat fly? Often, bats fly unsteadily with their mouths open. Although this may make them look sinister, it is not a sign that they are poised to attack. Rather, bats are using echolocation to find food. Echolocation works just like your voice when you yell and hear your echo. As bats fly, they make high-pitched clicking sounds with their noses and mouths. These sounds echo, or bounce, off whatever they meet. By listening for the echoes, bats can determine their surroundings and whether prey is present. By reading the echo, bats know an object's size, texture, density, and distance. Indeed, bats are fascinating creatures that certainly do more good than harm.

QUESTIONS

1. Which of the following would be the best title for this passage?

- A. Bats Are Our Friends
- B. Beware of Bats
- C. Those Cute and Furry Creatures
- D. The Truth About Bats

2. Which of the following best states the author's purpose?

- A. to inform the reader about vampire bats
- B. to dispel myths about bats
- C. to persuade readers to protect bats
- D. to tell a story about bats

3. Which of the following statements best describes the reason for the last paragraph?

- A. It explains why bats fly unsteadily.
- B. It defines echolocation.
- C. It explains one of bats' fascinating skills.
- D. It compares people to bats.

4. According to the passage, why do many people fear bats?

- A. Myths and stories have portrayed bats inaccurately.
- B. Vampire bats have been known to attack people.
- C. Bats are mysterious and fly only at night.
- D. People fear what they do not understand.

5. As used in the passage, the word *sustenance* most nearly means

- A. fluids.
- B. nesting materials.
- C. skills.
- D. nourishment.

6. Which of the following is NOT a reason explaining how bats help people?

- A. They kill large numbers of mosquitoes, which are obviously pests.
- B. They are used to make medicines.
- C. They enable plant reproduction by carrying pollen from flower to flower.
- D. They have helped scientists learn about echolocation.

DIRECTIONS: *Read the passage and answer the questions that follow it.*

Mummification

Tʜᴇ ᴀɴᴄɪᴇɴᴛ Eɢʏᴘᴛɪᴀɴs are known for their careful methods of mummification. They carried out this important ritual because they believed that the person's ka, or life force, would exist in the afterlife only if it had a body in which to live. After an important person died, usually a pharaoh, the process would begin.

Mummifying a body could take up to seventy days. First, the body would be purified with wine and water from the Nile. Then an **incision** was made on the left side of the body so the internal organs could be removed. The vital organs (liver, stomach, intestines, and lungs) were preserved. The brain was removed through the nose and thrown away. The heart was kept in the middle of the chest because it was thought to be the center of intelligence. Originally, the vital organs would be placed in special jars that were placed in the tomb with the body, but in later practices, they were wrapped and put back into the body.

Next, the body was covered with a special salt solution and left to dehydrate for almost forty days. It was washed again and rubbed with oils and herbs before being wrapped with layers of linen. Special charms were often put between the layers of cloth to protect the person during his or her journey through the underworld. During this process, a priest would often say prayers to keep evil spirits away.

When the wrapping was finished, the mummy was put in a coffin, and a funeral was held. The body was then placed in a tomb alongside special, valuable objects, such as furniture, clothing, and jewels. People also put food and drink in the tomb for use in the afterlife. After all this preparation, the body would finally be ready to make its journey through the underworld. ◐

QUESTIONS

1. Which of the following would be the best title for this passage?
   A. Different Funeral Rituals
   B. Preserving the Life Force
   C. Egyptian Superstitions
   D. Living Like an Egyptian

2. Which of the following best states the author's purpose?
   A. to explain how the Egyptians lived
   B. to show how a religious ceremony has significant meaning
   C. to explain why mummies are frightening
   D. to explain the process and reasons for mummification

3. Which of the following best describes how the Egyptians viewed vital organs?
   A. Organs were not needed in the afterlife because the person was dead.
   B. Only the vital organs were preserved.
   C. All organs were seen as "vital" and were kept inside the body during mummification.
   D. The ancient Egyptians lacked knowledge about organ function and medical procedures.

4. As used in the passage, the word *incision* means
   A. cut.
   B. diagram.
   C. bandage.
   D. stitch.

5. Which of the following best describes the reason for the last paragraph?
   A. to show how little trouble people go through when someone dies
   B. to explain the process of mummification
   C. to show how the Egyptians prepared a person for the afterlife
   D. to prove there is life after death

6. Which series best explains the process of mummification?
   A. purification, dehydration, wrapping, burial
   B. removing the organs, wrapping, dehydration, burial
   C. wrapping with linen, removing the brain, dehydration, burial
   D. removing the organs, cleaning the body, burial, dehydration

DIRECTIONS: *Read the passage and answer the questions that follow it.*

First Female in Flight

URING THE 1920s AND 1930s, America was captivated by airplanes and the concept of flying. As in many other professions, men dominated the field of aviation during this era. This changed, however, when Amelia Earhart became the first woman to set **aviation** records.

Amelia Earhart was born in Atchison, Kansas, in 1897. Fascinated by women who worked in difficult professions, Earhart would keep articles about successful women. In 1928, a New York publisher named George Putnam asked Earhart if she wanted to fly with him. Their journey from Newfoundland to Wales made Earhart the first woman to fly in an airplane over the Atlantic Ocean. Later, in 1932, Earhart made the journey by herself, setting another record for women. Amelia Earhart wrote two books about these flights: *20 Hours, 40 Minutes* (1928) and *The Fun of It* (1932). Earhart set many other aviation records in her time, but she is best remembered for attempting to fly around the world. During this trip in 1937, she and her navigator, Frederick Noonan, disappeared somewhere between New Guinea and Howland Island in the Pacific Ocean. Neither their plane nor their bodies have ever been found.

Amelia Earhart had used her career as a famous pilot to advance the causes she believed in: establishing commercial airlines and improving the status of women. Earhart served as the president of an organization of women pilots called the Ninety-Nines. She used her aviation records and literature to spread the message that flying would soon be a part of daily life. To the public, she identified herself as a feminist. In 1931, Earhart married Putnam, but she planned never to have children. Earhart's legacy, however, lives on through her contributions to women's history and aviation. ●

QUESTIONS

1. **With which of the following statements would Amelia Earhart most likely agree?**
   A. It is very difficult to prove your doubters wrong.
   B. All women have the right to pursue their goals.
   C. Flying is the greatest human accomplishment ever.
   D. If Earhart had trained a little more, she would not have disappeared with her plane.

2. **As used in the passage, the word *aviation* most nearly means**
   A. flying.
   B. cleaning.
   C. working.
   D. writing.

3. **Which of the following best states the author's purpose?**
   A. to show how women should stay at home and raise children
   B. to explain why Earhart's body has never been found
   C. to explain why Earhart is famous
   D. to show how dangerous it is to fly

4. **Which of the following statements best describes the reason for the second paragraph?**
   A. It explains Earhart's aviation career and records.
   B. It gives the details about Earhart's personal life.
   C. It proves Earhart was a successful author.
   D. It explains where Earhart and her co-pilot disappeared.

5. **According to the passage, how did Earhart use her fame?**
   A. Earhart used her fame to become rich.
   B. Earhart used her fame to bring attention to aviation and feminism.
   C. Earhart used her fame to fund her children's education.
   D. Earhart used her fame to become a successful author.

6. **Which of the following statements is true?**
   A. Earhart married her publisher and became a successful author.
   B. Earhart died on a solo flight across the Pacific Ocean.
   C. Earhart was a feminist who worked for a commercial airline.
   D. Earhart was the first woman to fly solo across the Atlantic Ocean.

DIRECTIONS: *Read the passage and answer the questions that follow it.*

The Black Widow

THE BLACK WIDOW lives in warmer regions of the world, including all four deserts in the southwestern United States. It is considered to be one of the most venomous spiders in North America; however, only the female black widow is poisonous. The venom she **excretes** is fifteen times more poisonous than that of a rattlesnake. Even though the amount of venom secreted by a black widow is minuscule, it can still be fatal.

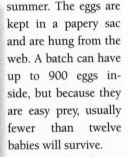

The female black widow has a reddish hourglass marking on the underside of her abdomen. The males have yellow and red bands and spots on their backs. Both have shiny black bodies, and the females, with bodies about an inch and a half long, are twice the size of males. Hatchlings are usually white or yellowish-white before they turn black. Before they are fully mature, both sexes look like the male spider and are not poisonous.

These spiders usually mate during the spring. Sometimes, the female has been known to kill and eat the male after they mate. The female can lay up to nine batches of eggs during one summer. The eggs are kept in a papery sac and are hung from the web. A batch can have up to 900 eggs inside, but because they are easy prey, usually fewer than twelve babies will survive.

The black widow is shy and likes to live on the undersides of rocks, plants, and other places where webs can be built. They hang upside down from the web, which does not have a special structure or form. After the black widow catches insects in its web, it makes small holes in the prey and sucks out the liquid from its body. This vampire-like behavior could be one reason why people are fearful of spiders. ◗

QUESTIONS

1. Which of the following would be the best title for this passage?

   A. Beware of Spiders

   B. How to Treat a Spider Bite

   C. Black Widow Revealed

   D. Arachnophobia

2. Which of the following best states the author's purpose?

   A. to make more people afraid of spiders

   B. to explain how the black widow lives

   C. to show how spiders help keep the insect population low

   D. to describe how vicious the female black widow can be

3. Which statement best describes the reason for the last paragraph?

   A. to show how the black widow is like a vampire

   B. to show how cute spiders are

   C. to describe how the female lays its eggs

   D. to describe the black widow's habitat and eating habits

4. Which word best describes the mating behavior of the black widow?

   A. hideous

   B. cannibalistic

   C. unfair

   D. gross

5. As used in the passage, the word *excretes* most nearly means

   A. injects.

   B. absorbs.

   C. vomits.

   D. holds.

6. Which description of the black widow is true?

   A. The male spider is larger but weaker than the female.

   B. The female is larger than the male and is poisonous.

   C. The male spider lays egg sacs that contain up to 900 babies.

   D. The male spider kills and eats the female after mating.

DIRECTIONS: *Read the passage and answer the questions that follow it.*

Floods

RIVERS ARE OFTEN APPRECIATED for their beauty and the benefits they offer to humans and wildlife; however, rivers can also be deadly and destructive in the event of a flood. Floods are violent forces of nature that can destroy homes, buildings, roads, and crops. They can also kill animals and people. While most floods are harmful, it is important to point out that some are beneficial. When the Nile floods, for example, **fertile** soil is washed ashore. This soil contains essential nutrients that help crops grow.

When heavy rains occur, sometimes too much water runs into a river. This causes the river to rise over its banks and flood. River floods usually happen in the spring when heavy rains melt snow. The rain and snow together are often too much for the river to handle. Heavy rainstorms, like those that occur during hurricanes and typhoons, also cause flooding. These storms, which originate over the ocean, can bring massive quantities of water to the land very quickly. When the rivers cannot carry the rains away fast enough, the land floods. Other rainstorms, such as cloudbursts, also cause floods. A cloudburst is a heavy rainstorm that lasts only an hour or two. Because a large amount of water falls in a short time, the ground does not have enough time to absorb it. The water then flows into creeks, streams, and rivers downstream. This is called a flash flood because the flood happens and disappears quickly. These floods are especially dangerous because people have no chance to prepare or escape.

Rivers are not the only cause of floods. Ocean floods can happen when winds blow large waves toward the land. These massive waves bring a large volume of water to the shore and cause flooding. Volcanoes can also cause flooding when an eruption melts ice and snow. Regardless of their causes, floods are truly powerful forces that can bring both devastation and rebirth to the land. ●

QUESTIONS

1. **Which of the following would be the best title for this passage?**
   A. Floods Are Our Friends
   B. Rain, Wind, Water, and Floods
   C. Planning for a Flood
   D. Calm Waters

2. **Which of the following best states the author's purpose?**
   A. to explain how a flood happens
   B. to show how dangerous floods can be
   C. to show how floods benefit farmers
   D. to show how only rivers cause flood damage

3. **Which of the following statements best describes the reason for the second paragraph?**
   A. It explains why floods only happen in the spring.
   B. It explains how cloudbursts are formed.
   C. It explains why flash floods are so dangerous.
   D. It explains how different storms cause rivers to flood.

4. **As used in the passage, the word *fertile* most nearly means**
   A. harmful.
   B. heavy.
   C. rich.
   D. poor.

5. **According to the passage, how does a flood form?**
   A. A flood occurs when a riverbank overflows or the land cannot absorb rainfall.
   B. A flood occurs when too much rain fills the ocean.
   C. A flood occurs in the spring, when ocean tides are highest.
   D. A flood occurs when there is not enough water in a riverbank.

6. **According to the passage, which of the following statements is true?**
   A. Floods produce more benefits than destruction.
   B. Flash floods are dangerous because people cannot prepare for them.
   C. Volcanic eruptions cannot cause flooding.
   D. Rivers are always dangerous bodies of water.

DIRECTIONS: *Read the passage and answer the questions that follow it.*

Chocolate

WHILE MANY CHOCOLATE candies are available in the United States today, we are not the first to eat this tasty treat. The word "chocolate" is a Nahuatl word. Nahuatl is a language that originated almost 500 years ago with the Aztecs. Many people in Mexico still speak it today. The Aztecs believed that chocolate was a gift from the gods and that the cacao trees were bridges between earth and heaven. Chocolate was used for daily drinks and also for special ceremonies.

When Spaniards came to Mexico in the 1500s, they were introduced to the Aztec's chocolate and learned how it was made. Chocolate is made from the cacao bean. The beans grow in pods on trees. The seeds are removed from the pods and left to ferment. Then, the seeds are dried, roasted, and ground into small pieces. When the seeds are ground, oil, called cocoa butter, is released. This butter is mixed with the ground pieces to form chocolate liquor, which is then left to cool and harden. Chocolate liquor is the base for all chocolate products. If sugar is not added, the chocolate stays bitter. Milk chocolate is made when milk and sugar are added to the liquor. Cocoa powder is made when the liquor is ground into powder, and often the powder is mixed with milk and sugar to make a hot drink.

The Spaniards learned these processes and wrote about them in a book called *History of the Indies,* which was translated into English in 1604. The rest of Europe soon became fascinated with chocolate, but it was not until 1657 that it became available in a candy shop in London, England. Since chocolate was new in this part of the world, it was a **luxury** item. Later, other countries discovered the tasty treat, and soon, people like Milton S. Hershey made chocolate affordable and available to the public. **o**

QUESTIONS

1. Which of the following would be the best title for this passage?

   A. Aztec Treats

   B. The Spanish Invasion of Mexico

   C. From Cacao to Chocolate

   D. Nahuatl Influences

2. Which of the following best states the author's purpose?

   A. to show how the Spanish robbed from the Aztecs

   B. to show how chocolate is enjoyed all over the world today

   C. to explain where the word "chocolate" comes from

   D. to show where chocolate came from and how it is made

3. As used in the passage, the word *luxury* most nearly means

   A. expensive.

   B. affordable.

   C. royal.

   D. tasty.

4. Which of the following statements best describes the reason for the first paragraph?

   A. It explains the origin of chocolate and how it was used.

   B. It shows how the Nahuatl language is no longer used today.

   C. It explains how the Aztecs misused the cacao bean.

   D. It explains where the word "chocolate" comes from.

5. According to the passage, how is chocolate made?

   A. Beans from the cacao plant are ground into liquor and used for drinks and candies.

   B. Beans from the cacao plant are dried, roasted, and ground to make chocolate.

   C. Beans from the cacao plant are ground into powder and left to dry before using for drinks and candies.

   D. Beans from the cacao plant are soaked in liquor then left to dry before being ground into powder.

6. How did the Aztecs view chocolate?

   A. The Aztecs used chocolate only in special ceremonies.

   B. The Aztecs believed that chocolate was a temptation from evil demons.

   C. The Aztecs drank chocolate daily and thought it was divine.

   D. The Aztecs hated chocolate because it was bitter.

DIRECTIONS: *Read the passage and answer the questions that follow it.*

The Battle for Land

Before European settlers came to America, Native American tribes lived on the land, establishing their own customs, religions, and government. The Cherokee Nation lived in the eastern part of the country, around the Appalachian Mountains. They hunted, fished, and farmed in the states we now call Virginia, West Virginia, Kentucky, Tennessee, the Carolinas, Mississippi, and Georgia. More and more European settlers migrated to these regions of America during the 1700s and 1800s. These new settlers soon caused problems for the Native Americans.

Because the Native Americans, also called Indians, did not do things the way the Europeans did, they were regarded as "savages." President Thomas Jefferson thought that the Indians should be "civilized," or converted to Christianity and forced to follow European customs. The Native Americans built European-style homes and farms, created a written language, and wrote a constitution, but many of the Europeans still did not want to cooperate with them. Since the Europeans wanted the Native Americans' land, political leaders used the government to take it from the Indians.

The U.S. government recognized the Cherokee Nation as a nation with its own laws and customs, but the U.S. did not protect the Cherokees' rights. The Indians battled the Supreme Court over the land, but they were forced to move. During the 1820s, 1830s, and 1840s, the U.S. government forced the Native Americans to move from their homes to areas hundreds of miles away. President Andrew Jackson and President Martin Van Buren used policies, such as the Indian Removal Act, to force the Cherokee Nation to give up its land east of the Mississippi River. The U.S. Army gathered the Indians, put them into **internment** camps, and forced them to move. Their journey to the Indian Territory was called the Trail of Tears because many Indians died from hunger, disease, and exhaustion. No wonder the Native American population and the rich cultures of various Native American nations were tragically affected. ○

QUESTIONS

1. How does the author feel about the relocation of the Native Americans?
   A. The author remains objective about the situation.
   B. The author feels it was unstoppable.
   C. The author feels it was a tragedy.
   D. The author owns land that once belonged to the Cherokee.

2. Which of the following best states the author's purpose?
   A. to inform the reader about Native American customs
   B. to show the strength of the U.S. Army
   C. to explain how Indians and Europeans lived together peacefully
   D. to describe how the Cherokee Nation lost its land

3. Which of the following statements best describes the reason for the second paragraph?
   A. It shows how much the Indians hated the Europeans.
   B. It explains Native American religious customs.
   C. It describes how the Indians tried to live peacefully with the Europeans.
   D. It describes Thomas Jefferson's political career.

4. As used in the passage, the word *internment* most nearly means
   A. summer.
   B. prison.
   C. voluntary.
   D. friendly.

5. According to the passage, why was the Cherokee Nation forced to move?
   A. because the settlers wanted their land
   B. because Thomas Jefferson told them to
   C. because the land was not good for farming or hunting
   D. because the settlers' diseases were killing the Cherokee

6. *Answer the following question using complete sentences:*
   Did the U.S. government have the right to take the land from the Native Americans? Why or why not?

DIRECTIONS: *Read the passage and answer the questions that follow it.*

Volcanoes

VOLCANOES ARE PERFECT examples of nature's awesome power. A volcano is a mountain with an open summit with vents that extend down to **molten** rock beneath the earth's surface. Through this vent, gases, ash, and molten rock are expelled. Molten rock, or magma, is made of large amounts of gases and water vapor. When the magma pours onto the earth's surface as hot, red, oozing liquid, it is called lava.

As the magma rises to the earth's surface, the gases it contains try to escape. This causes great pressure that eventually forces the ground to rupture. Then, the magma's gases push massive amounts of dust and ash into the air. Tons of ash form a tall cone around the volcano's vent, and lava pours out. The build-up of ash and lava over the course of many years forms the volcano. In this way, a volcano is different from other mountains because it is not formed by the upward motion of the earth's crust.

Most volcanoes were formed millions of years ago, but some have formed recently. They are usually found in areas called volcanic belts. One large belt of active volcanoes in the Pacific Ocean is called the Ring of Fire. This area is home to seventy-five percent of the world's active and dormant volcanoes. The Ring of Fire supports so many volcanoes because it borders the intersection of several of Earth's plates. These plates are like rafts of rock beneath the earth's surface that slide along, bump into, and cross over other plates. Beneath these plates, magma pushes upwards and forms new crust. When the magma tries to escape, volcanoes begin to form. ●

QUESTIONS

1. **What would be the best title for this passage?**
   - **A.** Ring of Fire
   - **B.** Cold Magma
   - **C.** Uncovering Volcanoes
   - **D.** Fleeing from Danger

2. **As used in the passage, the word _molten_ most nearly means**
   - **A.** melted.
   - **B.** frozen.
   - **C.** hard.
   - **D.** moldy.

3. **Which best describes the reason for the last paragraph?**
   - **A.** It describes only the Ring of Fire.
   - **B.** It shows how plates help in creating volcanoes.
   - **C.** It explains why there are no active volcanoes today.
   - **D.** It explains why there are no volcanoes in the U.S.

4. **Which of the following best states the author's purpose?**
   - **A.** to describe the difference between magma and lava
   - **B.** to show how volcanoes are ancient creations that have no importance today
   - **C.** to show the process of volcano formation
   - **D.** to tell the ancient myths about volcanic formation

5. **According to the passage, what is the first step of volcano formation?**
   - **A.** Volcanoes are formed when lava erupts from a mountain.
   - **B.** Volcanoes are formed when magma causes pressure under the surface.
   - **C.** Volcanoes are formed when plates under the ocean move apart.
   - **D.** Volcanoes are formed when cones of ash form aboveground.

6. **Which word might best describe the actions of a volcano?**
   - **A.** hot
   - **B.** unimportant
   - **C.** calm
   - **D.** violent

DIRECTIONS: *Read the passage and answer the questions that follow it.*

Judo

IMAGINE BEING ABLE to defend yourself from an attacker without needing to strike a blow or use weapons. This is the basic principle of the sport of judo, which means "gentle way" in Japanese. Jigoro Kano developed judo in 1882, based on an ancient hand-to-hand fighting style called *jujitsu.*

Judo has also become a popular sport in countries other than Japan, including the U.S. During training and competitions, judo students wear a white jacket and pants. The loose-fitting jacket is held in place with a belt, the color of which indicates a student's skill level. As beginners, competitors wear white belts. When they have reached the highest skill level, they wear black belts. The different levels in between are represented by other belt colors. Reaching a new belt level requires substantial training and competition. Judo students compete in two ways: *randori* and *kata.* In *randori,* competitors can use free combat; in *kata,* fighters use planned movements.

In competitions, and if they were attacked on the street, judo experts are able to overcome people larger and stronger than they are. This is possible because the sport of judo focuses on self-defense by using **nonresistance** and leverage to knock opponents off balance. In other words, judo fighters use their opponents' own moves and force against them. Once this happens, they can overcome attackers using two techniques: throws and locks. Throws are named for the body parts involved in the move (hand, foot, shoulder, etc.). Locks are used on the legs, arms, and neck to keep the opponent from moving. Because these moves can be dangerous, anyone interested in learning judo should train with an instructor. Above all, the art of judo is a way of life, of yielding or giving way in order to succeed. As such, judo is never used to overpower others, but rather to let them defeat themselves. ●

QUESTIONS

1. Which of the following would be the best title for this passage?
   A. Ancient Sports
   B. Kata
   C. The Gentle Way
   D. Hand-to-Hand Combat

2. Which of the following best states the author's purpose?
   A. to show how using weapons is the best way to win a fight
   B. to show how important belt ranking is in judo
   C. to describe the difference between locks and throws
   D. to describe the sport of judo

3. As used in the passage, the word *nonresistance* most nearly means
   A. nonviolence.
   B. physical force.
   C. punches.
   D. weapons.

4. Which of the following best describes the reason for the last paragraph?
   A. It describes the difference between judo and jujitsu.
   B. It describes how judo experts combat opponents.
   C. It describes how judo fighters use their weapons.
   D. It describes how judo fighters' methods of nonresistance do not work.

5. According to the passage, what type of sport is judo?
   A. Judo is a hand-to-hand combat sport.
   B. Judo is an ancient Japanese fighting technique.
   C. Judo is a self-defense sport.
   D. Judo is practiced with weapons.

6. Which of the following statements best describes the reason for the second paragraph?
   A. It shows how only the Japanese practice judo.
   B. It explains the many attack methods of judo students.
   C. It shows how judo students compete.
   D. It shows how judo students are ranked.

DIRECTIONS: *Read the passage and answer the questions that follow it.*

The Nose

ALTHOUGH IT IS often overlooked, the nose is an amazing organ that serves two important functions: breathing and smelling. The outside of the nose, or the external nose, is the visible part on the face. The external nose has two openings, called nostrils, which are separated by the septum. The lower section of the septum is made of cartilage; the upper is made of bone. The internal nose is hollow and is located above the mouth. The septum bone divides the inner nose into two sides. The internal nose extends from the nostrils to a part of the throat, called the pharynx.

The nose filters dust and foreign particles from the air that you breathe. Lined with tiny hairs, called cilia, the nostrils function partly to trap large particles in the air. The nostrils are also lined with a mucous membrane. This membrane produces sticky fluid, called mucus, to trap the smaller particles.

Mucus and dust particles make up the substance you see after blowing your nose. The mucous membrane contains many blood vessels, called capillaries. The blood that passes through these capillaries keeps the mucous membrane the same temperature as the rest of the body. When air passes through the nose, the membrane warms and moistens the air.

In the upper portion of the inner nose are olfactory cells. These "smelling" cells are connected by nerves to your brain; together, they work to give you the sense of smell. When you inhale, molecules enter your nose. Then, the molecules come into contact with the olfactory cells. Finally, the nerves carry the messages to the brain where the **odor** is interpreted. Overall, while it may seem fairly simple, the nose actually plays a very important, complex role. **O**

QUESTIONS

1. **Which of the following would be the best title for this passage?**
   A. Silly Cilia
   B. Basic Breathing
   C. How Do You Smell?
   D. Olfactory Works

2. **Which of the following best states the author's purpose?**
   A. to show how important the senses are
   B. to show how the sense of smell affects the taste of food
   C. to describe how the mucous membrane works
   D. to describe how the nose helps us breathe and smell

3. **What is the purpose of the second paragraph?**
   A. It describes the purpose of the internal nose.
   B. It describes the nose's filtering process.
   C. It describes the formation of mucus.
   D. It describes the function of cilia.

4. **Which statement about the external nose is true?**
   A. The external nose is where mucus forms.
   B. The external nose is separated by the pharynx.
   C. The external nose traps dust particles.
   D. The external nose is made of cartilage and bone.

5. **As used in the passage, the word *odor* most nearly means**
   A. smell.
   B. cell.
   C. chemical.
   D. information.

6. **What does the mucous membrane do?**
   A. The mucous membrane heats the air and pushes out dust.
   B. The mucous membrane cools the air and traps dust.
   C. The mucous membrane traps dust and warms the air.
   D. The mucous membrane makes mucus.

DIRECTIONS: *Read the passage and answer the questions that follow it.*

César Chávez:
Heroic Figure

AT THE AGE OF TEN, César Chávez quit school to become a migrant farm worker. His parents had lost their farm during the Great Depression, and he worked to help support his family. His experiences in vineyards opened his eyes to the numerous problems faced by farm workers. Eventually, he became a leader in the fight against the low wages and poor working conditions that fellow workers were facing. In 1962, Chávez formed the National Farm Workers Association (now known as the United Farm Workers). This group worked towards improving the treatment of farm workers. A firm believer in non-violent protest, Chávez practiced the principles of Gandhi and Dr. Martin Luther King, Jr., to achieve his goals. During the 1970s, the UFW held strikes and boycotted grapes and lettuce to get better wages for the growers. In the 1980s, Chávez fasted to protest the use of dangerous **pesticides** on grapes.

Such movements were highly effective in drawing national attention, and the hard work resulted in industry-wide contracts and new legislation.

Through numerous efforts and achievements, César Chávez led the first successful farm workers union in American history. His brave efforts provided thousands of farmers with fair wages, medical coverage, benefits, and legal protections that they did not have before.

Although Chávez did not have a formal education past the eighth grade and never made more than $6,000 a year, he was a widely respected man. Chávez's dedication to social justice has been celebrated in various ways: buildings have been named after him, his birthday is celebrated as a holiday, scholarships have been established in his name, and a foundation was created to carry out his legacy. In fact, Senator Kennedy called him "one of the heroic figures of our time." ●

QUESTIONS

1. **Why was César Chávez important?**
   A. Senator Kennedy recognized his efforts.
   B. He had a good philosophy of life.
   C. He fought to provide protections to farm workers.
   D. He sacrificed his education to help his impoverished family.

2. **How did César Chávez mimic Gandhi and Dr. King?**
   A. through fasting, holding strikes, and starting boycotts
   B. by dropping out of school
   C. by creating legislation to protect workers
   D. by working the fields

3. **The author most likely chose to write about César Chávez in order to**
   A. show how unfair the world can be.
   B. provide a reason for people to stop complaining about their own difficulties.
   C. show how money helps people accomplish their dreams.
   D. provide an example of what determination and hard work can do for people.

4. **What impact did César Chávez have on America?**
   A. He had no impact because he did not live in America.
   B. He is the most important figure in American history.
   C. His legacy has been widely recognized and celebrated.
   D. He is only important in the legislative arena.

5. **As used in the passage, the word *pesticides* most nearly means**
   A. chemicals.
   B. insects.
   C. irrigation methods.
   D. soil.

6. *Answer the following question using complete sentences:*
   How do you think César Chávez was able to achieve so much, given his status as an impoverished migrant farmer with little formal education?

DIRECTIONS: *Read the passage and answer the questions that follow it.*

All Hail the Queen

QUEEN LATIFAH, whose birth name is Dana Elaine Owens, has been called hip-hop's first lady because of her empowering song lyrics. She was born in Newark, New Jersey, on March 18, 1970. Her mother was a teacher, and her father and brother were both police officers.

Latifah began her working career as a Burger King employee but soon got into the music industry by being a human beatbox, or imitating the sound of a drum, in the rap group Ladies Fresh. At the age of eighteen, Latifah released her first album, *Wrath of My Madness*. Queen Latifah was unhappy with the **misogynistic** lyrics produced by the popular male performers at the time, so she decided to create lyrics that appeal to both genders.

Queen Latifah has been one of the greatest hip-hop artists of the decade, but this has not been her only focus. Her career spans the entertainment industry. Queen Latifah has performed in numerous films and appeared on television shows. She also manages her own company, Flavor Unit. Her experience has led to wide recognition. She was the first female rapper to be nominated for an Academy Award, she was ranked number 72 on VH1's 100 Greatest Women of Rock-N-Roll, and in January of 2006, she was the first hip-hop artist to be given a star on the Hollywood Walk of Fame. These are just some of her awards. While her nickname "Latifah" is Arabic for delicate and sensitive, her music and her manner are strong, empowered, and wise. ●

QUESTIONS

1. Which of the following statements is a fact?

　　A. Queen Latifah is one of the greatest hip-hop artists alive today.

　　B. Queen Latifah was the first female rapper to be nominated for an Academy Award.

　　C. Queen Latifah is one of the greatest women of rock-n-roll.

　　D. Queen Latifah is strong, empowered, and wise.

2. Which of the following best states the author's purpose?

　　A. to show how many African-American artists are in the music industry

　　B. to show how changing your name can help your career

　　C. to describe the successful career of a female hip-hop artist

　　D. to show why Queen Latifah should have become a police officer

3. As used in the passage, the word *misogynistic* most nearly means

　　A. sexist.

　　B. superior.

　　C. upbeat.

　　D. popular.

4. Which of the following statements best describes Queen Latifah's career?

　　A. The highest point of her career was the release of her first album.

　　B. Latifah is trying to make new strides in the entertainment industry but is facing problems because of her gender and race.

　　C. As a female, she is having problems keeping up with male artists.

　　D. Latifah's career continues to grow, and she has achieved success in different areas of the entertainment industry.

5. Which of the following best describes the reason for the second paragraph?

　　A. It shows how Latifah got into the music industry.

　　B. It explains the meaning of her nickname.

　　C. It names Latifah's first album.

　　D. It describes her family life.

6. To what might the author be alluding in the final sentence of the passage?

　　A. Latifah is rough and insensitive in her song lyrics.

　　B. Latifah is a strong female artist who empowers her listeners.

　　C. Latifah is Arabic, not African-American.

　　D. The author is comparing Latifah to a flower.

DIRECTIONS: *Read the passage and answer the questions that follow it.*

Earthquakes

As I turned the corner, around a frame house, there was a great rattle and jar, and it occurred to me that here was an item! —no doubt a fight in that house. Before I could turn and seek the door, there came a terrific shock; the ground seemed to roll under me in waves, interrupted by a violent joggling up and down, and there was a heavy grinding noise as of brick houses rubbing together. I fell up against the frame house and hurt my elbow. I knew what it was now... a third and still severer shock came, and as I reeled about on the pavement trying to keep my footing, I saw a sight! The entire front of a tall four-story brick building on Third Street sprung outward like a door and fell sprawling across the street, raising a great dust-like volume of smoke!

-Mark Twain

THE STORY EXCERPT above is from *Roughing It,* a novel Mark Twain wrote in 1865 while he lived in San Francisco. Twain describes his experience with an earthquake, or the violent movement in the Earth's crust that results from pressure building underground. Earthquakes are the result of movement among the tectonic plates in the Earth's crust. If these plates collide, slide past, or move away from each other, pressure builds. This pressure can develop over a period of many years, becoming stronger as time passes. When the pressure becomes too strong for the plates to handle, the rock breaks, and the Earth shakes. Earthquakes that occur under the ocean can cause dangerous **tsunamis** to engulf the shore and areas inland.

There are approximately 150,000 earthquakes each year, but only about 100 actually cause damage to human-made structures. Most earthquakes are so mild that people do not even notice them; they are detected only with a seismograph, a scientific instrument that measures movement in the Earth's crust. Some areas are more susceptible to earthquakes than others because they are located near fault lines, areas where the tectonic plates meet. Because of San Francisco's proximity to the San Andreas Fault, Twain's experience there is not an uncommon one, quakes having been experienced by millions of people in and around that particular fault for centuries. ○

QUESTIONS

1. Which of the following would be the best title for this passage?
- **A.** Twain's Adventures
- **B.** Below the Ground
- **C.** Preparing for Disaster
- **D.** Tsunamis

2. As used in the passage, the word *tsunamis* most nearly means
- **A.** large waves.
- **B.** sand blasts.
- **C.** sea creatures.
- **D.** sunken ships.

3. Which of the following best states the author's purpose?
- **A.** to give a famous literary figure the opportunity to discuss a natural disaster
- **B.** to describe how earthquakes happen
- **C.** to show why some areas have more earthquakes than others
- **D.** to prove that earthquakes are harmful to people

4. Which group of adjectives best describes Twain's observations and emotions during the earthquake?
- **A.** noisy, safe, confused
- **B.** dangerous, exciting, calm
- **C.** loud, destructive, fearful
- **D.** confused, quiet, alone

5. Which of the following statements best describes the reason for the last paragraph?
- **A.** There is no reason to be fearful of destructive earthquakes.
- **B.** Earthquakes rarely happen, but when they do, the destruction they cause is completely unpredictable.
- **C.** Mark Twain left San Francisco because it is a dangerous place to live.
- **D.** While earthquakes happen almost daily, most are not strong enough to cause destruction.

6. According to the passage, how do earthquakes happen?
- **A.** The Earth's crust breaks open and land masses fall through the cracks after the plates below the ground move too far apart.
- **B.** When the plates below the Earth's surface are under too much pressure, they break and cause the ground above to shake.
- **C.** People and buildings put too much pressure on the Earth's surface, and this causes cracks in the ground.
- **D.** When the plates under the ocean move, large, destructive waves come ashore.

DIRECTIONS: *Read the passage and answer the questions that follow it.*

Rites of Passage

IMAGINE YOU ARE a ten-to-fourteen-year-old member of the Lakota Sioux. Upon speaking with the elders, you learn it is time for you to perform an important rite of passage: the vision quest. You must leave the tribe and venture into the woods alone for two to four days without clothing or food. After choosing an area that you feel is special, you must remain in a ten-foot circle and pray. During this time of fasting and **meditation**, you hope to receive a vision that will help guide you for the rest of your life. At the same time, you will also seek spiritual guidance from your god. Remain focused, however, because you might hallucinate from dehydration and hunger, or you may feel a strong urge to return home before you receive your vision. It is important to listen to all the elements of nature that surround you because they will provide the answer. After receiving your vision, choose an element, such as a rock or feather, to serve as a reminder,

protection, or guidance. Finally, return to the tribe for an interpretation of your vision and a celebration of recognition.

The vision quest is just one example of how a culture can recognize the important transitions that individuals make throughout their lives. Other transitional experiences include birth, adolescence, graduation, marriage, child bearing, and death. Ceremonies are performed to help people prepare for new roles they will be facing in society. It is believed that rites of passage have three phases: separation, limbo, and incorporation. During the separation phase, the person withdraws from his or her group to relocate to another area. After separating from the group, the person is in limbo, a physical and psychological transition, before reentering his or her group. From there, the individual grows and matures, demonstrating his or her advanced abilities and responsibilities.

●

QUESTIONS

1. **It can be inferred that the vision quest is a rite of passage during what time in a person's life?**
   A. birth
   B. marriage
   C. death
   D. adolescence

2. **As used in the passage, the word *meditation* most nearly means**
   A. anxiety.
   B. hallucination.
   C. deep focus.
   D. starvation.

3. **Which of the following statements best describes the reason for the second paragraph?**
   A. It explains how cultures celebrate rites of passage differently.
   B. It describes the transitional process individuals must go through.
   C. It defines the purpose of the vision quest.
   D. It lists the phases of life.

4. **Which of the following would be a good title for this passage?**
   A. How to Give Your Child Separation Anxiety
   B. Surviving the Wilderness
   C. Means of Transition
   D. Listening to Your Heart

5. **What is the goal of going on a vision quest?**
   A. to find important life answers
   B. to incorporate into a new tribe
   C. to lose weight
   D. to test your physical endurance

6. **Choose the answer that best describes the process of the vision quest.**
   A. feasting, meditating, receiving a vision, and separating from the tribe
   B. receiving a vision, praying, fasting, and leaving the tribe
   C. leaving the tribe, meditating, meeting with elders, and receiving a vision
   D. meeting with elders, leaving the tribe, praying, and receiving a vision

DIRECTIONS: *Read the passage and answer the questions that follow it.*

The Great Grand Canyon

THE GRAND CANYON is one of nature's most spectacular formations. Scientists believe that millions of years ago, this area was created by movement under the Earth's surface. When the area moved, the Colorado River and its tributaries started flowing and cutting through the layers of rock. As the river continued to move and flow, it **eroded** the rock, and deep gorges formed. Rain and strong winds caused the gorges to deepen. Some are as much as 5,000 feet deep.

The canyon is made up of many brightly colored cliffs, valleys, hills, and plateaus. The different colors on the rock walls mark different time periods in history. The layers at the bottom of the canyon could have been formed over one billion years ago. The plant and animal zones vary according to their depth in the canyon. The arid zone located closest to the river supports cacti, just like the desert. The zone at the top of the rim supports forests.

To protect the varied ecosystems and awesome beauty of the canyon, the United States designated the area as a National Park in 1919, and UNESCO added it to the list of World Heritage Sites in 1979. Tourists come to western Arizona year-round to visit the canyon. There, it is possible to hike the trails or ride a mule. Visitors also enjoy rafting, bird watching, fishing, horseback riding, and numerous other opportunities the park provides for tourists to view the beauty of the canyon and to observe the varied wildlife of this unique natural treasure. ●

QUESTIONS

1. Which of the following best states the author's purpose?

   A. to inform the reader about Arizona

   B. to describe the vegetation of the Grand Canyon

   C. to explain the history of the Grand Canyon

   D. to show how powerful water can be

2. Why was the Grand Canyon designated a National Park?

   A. to promote physical activity and healthy lifestyles

   B. to encourage tourism

   C. to create a beautiful recreation area

   D. to protect the ecosystems of the canyon

3. Which of the following statements best describes the reason for the second paragraph?

   A. It describes how the canyon is the same everywhere.

   B. It explains why some walls have different colors.

   C. It describes how the canyon was formed.

   D. It describes the different layers and zones of the canyon.

4. According to the passage, which statement best explains how the Grand Canyon was formed?

   A. The Grand Canyon was formed by wind and rain erosion.

   B. The Grand Canyon was formed when water eroded the rock.

   C. The Grand Canyon was formed by many earthquakes.

   D. The Grand Canyon was formed by heavy floods millions of years ago.

5. As used in the passage, the word *eroded* most nearly means

   A. wore away.

   B. built up.

   C. moved.

   D. left.

6. According to the passage, which of the following statements is true?

   A. The Grand Canyon began forming thousands of years ago.

   B. Acid rains helped erode the rock of the Grand Canyon.

   C. It is only possible to visit the Grand Canyon during the summer.

   D. The zone closest to the river is like a desert.

DIRECTIONS: *Read the passage and answer the questions that follow it.*

The WNBA

THE GAME OF BASKETBALL was created by James Naismith at the International YMCA Training School in January 1892, in Massachusetts. One month later, Sedna Berenson, the director of the gymnasium and an instructor of physical culture at Smith College, heard about the game and introduced new rules for female players that eliminated some of the sport's roughness. In March of 1893, she organized the first women's college basketball team; however, it took just over one hundred years for women's basketball to become a professional sport.

On April 24, 1996, the Women's National Basketball Association (WNBA) became official. The WNBA was scheduled to begin playing the following summer when there would be more airtime available to broadcast the games live. More than fifty million viewers watched the first season on the NBC, ESPN, and Lifetime Television networks. During the **inaugural** season, eight teams competed. By 2002, the WNBA expanded to sixteen teams comprising 176 professional women basketball players. In 2001, the games were broadcast to almost sixty million fans, in twenty-three different languages, and in 167 countries.

The WNBA is not only about the game, however, since players and the organization have established programs to benefit communities. One of their primary focuses is the "Read to Achieve" initiative, which promotes adult literacy and urges families to read to children. There are also youth basketball teams, the Jr. NBA and Jr. WNBA, which support and develop young players. The WNBA is also a partner of the National Alliance of Breast Cancer Organizations (NABCO). The WNBA is a dedicated organization that has come a long way since the game's creation. ⬤

QUESTIONS

1. What would be a good title for this passage?

   A. The Creation of the WNBA

   B. Women's Sports Still Lag Behind

   C. Shooting Hoops

   D. How to Improve Your Game

2. As mentioned in the passage, *inaugural* most nearly means

   A. failing.

   B. initial.

   C. political.

   D. exciting.

3. Which of the following best states the author's purpose?

   A. to show how women are gaining ground in sports

   B. to show how men still dominate professional sports

   C. to prove how sports teams can benefit society

   D. to tell the history of women's basketball

4. What can you infer about the last sentence of the first paragraph?

   A. Women's achievements in sports are often unrecognized.

   B. Money is often unavailable for both male and female teams.

   C. It was not possible for women to have their own team until this century.

   D. Historically, female athletes have had limited access to and participation in professional sports.

5. What is the author's purpose in the second paragraph?

   A. to demonstrate how far women's basketball has come in fewer than ten years

   B. to show that people will watch anything on television

   C. to show that sports have international appeal

   D. to highlight the partnership between broadcasters and sports teams

6. Why might the WNBA be partnered with the NABCO?

   A. because the cancer foundations always need more money, and the WNBA has the income to provide funding

   B. because Berenson died of breast cancer, and this was a way to remember her

   C. because breast cancer is a women's issue with which the athletes and viewers can identify

   D. because the league approved of the pink ribbons that symbolize breast cancer awareness

DIRECTIONS: *Read the passage and answer the questions that follow it.*

The Statue of Liberty

Give me your tired, your poor,
Your huddled masses yearning to breathe free,
The wretched refuse of your teeming shore.
Send these, the homeless tempest-tossed to me,
I lift my lamp beside the golden door!

-Emma Lazarus

THIS POETIC VERSE from the poem "The New Colossus" appears on the Statue of Liberty as a welcome to immigrants coming to America. The statue sits on Liberty Island in the New York Harbor, the place where many ships brought foreigners into America. In fact, the American Museum of Immigration is located inside the pedestal below the statue.

Formerly known as "Liberty Enlightening the World," the Statue of Liberty represents a woman holding a torch and a law book. The torch is being raised in her right hand. For years, the lighted torch helped many ships navigate the harbor. The tablet is held in her left hand with the date of the signing of the Declaration of Independence (July 4, 1776) **inscribed** on it.

The Statue of Liberty was a gift from the French. In 1865 a French historian, Édouard de Laboulaye, proposed the statue as a way to honor the alliance that was made between America and France during the American Revolution. The people of France contributed money to have the statue built. A French sculptor named Frédéric Auguste Bartholdi designed and sculpted the statue by hammering sheets of copper together by hand. The copper sheets were supported by a frame made of steel, which was designed by Gustave Eiffel, who also designed the Eiffel Tower, the best known monument in Europe.

When the statue was completed in 1885, it was taken apart, since it was too large to transport assembled, and sent by ship to the United States. When it was rebuilt, it was unveiled and dedicated by President Grover Cleveland on October 28, 1886. This statue is now one of America's most popular monuments. ●

QUESTIONS

1. Which of the following best states the author's purpose?
   A. to inform the reader about French sculptors and historians
   B. to discuss the Declaration of Independence
   C. to talk about world monuments
   D. to explain the significance of the Statue of Liberty

2. As used in the passage, the word *inscribed* most nearly means
   A. printed.
   B highlighted.
   C. removed.
   D. doodled.

3. Which of the following would be the best title for this passage?
   A. The French Are Our Friends
   B. A Gift From France
   C. Lady Liberty Leaves Home
   D. The Globe's Monuments

4. According to the passage, why is the Statue of Liberty important?
   A. It guides ships by serving as a lighthouse.
   B. It is a monument for Emma Lazarus's poem.
   C. It honors America's alliance with the French during the American Revolution.
   D. It represents America's determination to be a free nation.

5. Which of the following statements best describes the reason for the third paragraph? (Do not include the poem excerpt as a paragraph.)
   A. to describe how talented Americans are at making monuments
   B. to explain why the statue is important
   C. to describe how little time it took to build the statue
   D. to give the details about the statue's construction

6. *Answer the following question using complete sentences:*
   What do you think Emma Lazarus's poem means?

DIRECTIONS: *Read the passage and answer the questions that follow it.*

The Incas

THE INCAS WERE an ancient tribe of people who lived in South America. By the sixteenth century, their empire of more than one million people stretched from Ecuador to Chile. While the Incas conquered other tribes to expand their empire, the people who cooperated were treated well, and those who served as warriors for the Incas were greatly rewarded. Even though the Incas were an empire under one Inca, or ruler, each tribe was governed by its own group of elders. As the Incas conquered other territories, they educated each new territory's ruling-class children, they spread their belief that cooperation and contribution promote survival. They thought everyone should work for the good of everyone else.

Because the Incas lived in the Andes Mountains, it was difficult to farm. The people, however, were able to carve sections of the mountains and cultivate corn and potatoes. They were also masterful engineers who created massive forts, roads through mountains, bridges, aqueducts, and earth-drawings. Much of their work still exists today in almost perfect condition. The Incas were also very advanced in medicine and surgery, able to perform surgery on the skull successfully, for example.

Although this group of ancient peoples was advanced, they were defeated in 1535 by the Spanish conquistadors, who were led by Juan Francisco Pizarro. Pizarro's fierce army captured the emperor, Atahuallpa, and his family. The emperor offered Pizarro a ransom for his release, but Pizarro took the treasure and had Atahuallpa killed. Once the Inca and his family were destroyed, the empire fell quickly. Pizarro's army killed many of the Incas and stole vast amounts of gold, silver, and other treasures. The Incas were not able to survive against the conquistadors' foreign diseases, such as smallpox, and their advanced weapons. Unfortunately, the Incas were not the only native tribe that faced **demise** by foreigners. Many ancient cultures were ruined by the arrival of explorers from other parts of the world. ●

QUESTIONS

1. **Which of the following would be the best title for this passage?**
   A. Native of Mexico
   B. Juan Francisco Pizarro
   C. Fall of the Incas
   D. Ancient Times

2. **As used in the passage, the word *demise* most nearly means**
   A. death.
   B. victory.
   C. anguish.
   D. brutality.

3. **Which of the following statements best describes the reason for the last paragraph?**
   A. It gives one example of how the white men defeated the world.
   B. It explains how the Incas were defeated by the conquistadors.
   C. It tells how Pizarro was stealthy and untrustworthy.
   D. It shows how the Incas organized their own military.

4. **Which of the following best states the author's purpose?**
   A. to inform the reader about an ancient group of people
   B. to show how mixing different cultures can benefit society
   C. to give the history of South America
   D. to prove that more than one group of native tribes existed

5. **Which statement best describes the Incas?**
   A. The Incas were a non-religious group that made no contribution to greater society.
   B. The Incas were a small tribe that focused on agriculture and finding ways to irrigate their crops.
   C. The Incas were conquered by Pizarro because they had weak immune systems and ineffective weapons.
   D. The Incas were a vast empire that had advanced means of engineering, agriculture, and medicine.

6. **What idea can be inferred from the conclusion of the passage?**
   A. There are many people who have Inca ancestors.
   B. The conquistadors were a fierce militant group that sought world domination.
   C. Many native tribes no longer exist.
   D. It is good for foreign people to invade territories that do not belong to them.

DIRECTIONS: *Read the passage and answer the questions that follow it.*

Do Aliens Exist?

Do ALIENS EXIST? Could we truly be the only inhabitants of the universe? This debate has endured since ancient times. Many people believe they have seen unidentified flying objects (UFOs) or claim abduction by aliens. Those who believe there is life on other planets often argue that the government tries to hide or cover up the existence of UFOs.

A number of astronauts landed missions on the moon in the years 1969 through 1972. According to **unconfirmed** reports, several of these astronauts saw UFOs while in flight and after landing. They also claim that the astronauts saw flashing lights, domed buildings, and tracks on the moon's surface. These reports allege that alien crafts followed the astronauts' ships and that the domed buildings were part of an alien base on the moon. Other accounts state that the strange beings issued one or more warnings and do not want us, for any reason, to be on the moon. Maybe this explains why there have been no lunar landings in more than thirty years.

Furthermore, additional reports claim that NASA has not revealed all the evidence gathered from the lunar landings, nor has the organization released all the photographs and film taken during the lunar landings. Others contend that the lunar landings were a fraud, that they were photographed and filmed in Hollywood movie studios. If this is true, perhaps the government did it to hide evidence of alien life forms. Regardless, many speculate that the government, specifically the CIA, has proof of extraterrestrial life but is keeping it secret.

Why would anyone keep such proof secret? Would evidence of extraterrestrial life be so harmful? ●

QUESTIONS

1. **The author of the passage would most likely agree with which of the following statements?**
   A. The lunar landings were nothing more than Hollywood movies.
   B. All the astronauts who went to the moon know the truth about aliens.
   C. There are many theories about what the astronauts saw on the moon.
   D. Nothing unusual happened during the lunar landings.

2. **According to the passage, why is so little known about whether the astronauts truly saw UFOs?**
   A. Government agencies, such as the CIA, may be covering up the proof.
   B. Our government has been secretly working with aliens for centuries.
   C. The astronauts are not honest, and their claims are doubtful.
   D. Astronauts never even landed on the moon, so they could not have seen alien crafts.

3. **The tone of this passage would best be described as**
   A. cautionary.
   B. suspecting.
   C. disbelieving.
   D. angry.

4. **Which reason best describes why the author does not provide any quotations to support the points of the passage?**
   A. Providing quotations would make the passage less mysterious.
   B. The author wanted to finish the passage quickly, and quotations would have made it longer.
   C. Since the accounts of aliens are not proven, there are no appropriate quotations to support the passage.
   D. The author wants to make the reader think that the moon landings were a hoax.

5. **As used in the passage, the word *unconfirmed* most nearly means**
   A. not factual.
   B. unreliable.
   C. televised.
   D. radio broadcasted.

6. *Answer the following question using complete sentences:*
   Do you believe that aliens exist? Why or why not?

DIRECTIONS: *Read the passage and answer the questions that follow it.*

Mount Rushmore

THE FACES OF FOUR U.S. Presidents, memorialized in stone for their greatness, watch over America from a mountaintop in the Black Hills of South Dakota. This huge sculpture, called the Mount Rushmore National Memorial, features the faces of George Washington, Thomas Jefferson, Theodore Roosevelt, and Abraham Lincoln. Each **portrait** is sixty feet high and is visible from up to sixty miles away.

Gutzon Borglum, an American sculptor, designed and oversaw most of the work on Mount Rushmore. Before carving into the stone, Borglum made small models of the faces to serve as a guide. In 1927, Borglum and his many workers started the project, which took one million dollars and fourteen years to complete. Dynamite and drilling machines were used to carve the faces into the stone. Unfortunately, Borglum died before the memorial was finished, so his son continued his father's astounding project until funding was depleted in 1941.

The presidents whose faces appear on the side of the mountain were chosen because of their contributions in shaping America into the democratic country that it is today. George Washington was the first president and guided the creation of the nation. Thomas Jefferson drafted the words to the Declaration of Independence. This document asserted our independence and proclaimed that our nation was no longer under the rule of Great Britain. Abraham Lincoln played an important role in unifying the country into one nation that valued freedom and equality. Theodore Roosevelt led the United States during a time when America was becoming a world power. Through hard work, vision, and determination, Gutzon Borglum and his son immortalized these great leaders in a majestic setting for all the world to remember. ❍

QUESTIONS

1. **Which of the following would be the best title for this passage?**
   - **A.** Stonehenge
   - **B.** Faces on Rushmore
   - **C.** South Dakota
   - **D.** Stone Cold

2. **As used in the passage, the word *portrait* most nearly means**
   - **A.** face.
   - **B.** hill.
   - **C.** feature.
   - **D.** man.

3. **Which of the following best states the author's purpose?**
   - **A.** to describe how little importance Mount Rushmore really has
   - **B.** to attract people to South Dakota
   - **C.** to explain why Mount Rushmore was created
   - **D.** to give a brief history of American presidents

4. **Which of the following statements best describes the reason for the last paragraph?**
   - **A.** to explain why each president was chosen
   - **B.** to prove America's independence
   - **C.** to show that America is a world power
   - **D.** to tell how the U.S. values freedom and equality

5. **According to the passage, how was the memorial constructed?**
   - **A.** Mount Rushmore only took a few years to create.
   - **B.** Each face on Mount Rushmore was carved by hand.
   - **C.** The faces on Mount Rushmore were not constructed by humans.
   - **D.** Mount Rushmore was carved with the use of dynamite and special tools.

6. **Which of the following best describes Gutzon Borglum's role in creating the memorial on Mount Rushmore?**
   - **A.** Borglum made a drawing of Mount Rushmore and gave it to a crew to create.
   - **B.** Borglum wanted his face to be on the memorial since he designed it.
   - **C.** Borglum designed and helped carve Mount Rushmore.
   - **D.** Borglum estimated the timeline and budget for the project.

DIRECTIONS: *Read the passage and answer the questions that follow it.*

Tornadoes

IN THE CLASSIC MOVIE *The Wizard of Oz*, Dorothy and her dog, Toto, are swallowed by a tornado, taken far from their home in Kansas, and dropped in Oz. While Oz and Dorothy's story are fictional, the power of a tornado is not. Tornados are violent windstorms that can destroy homes, move heavy objects, and cause death or serious injuries. The winds made by a tornado are the most powerful on Earth. Tornadoes can whirl at speeds over 300 miles an hour. They can be several feet to over a mile wide and move forward at speeds around fifty miles an hour.

Tornadoes usually form in the late spring and summer. In thunderstorm-like weather, hot, moist air will rise quickly from the ground to the sky. The weather conditions above the ground cause this rising air to spin. The whirling air forms long, funnel-shaped wind storms that stretch from the clouds to the ground. The rising air inside the funnel moves very quickly and picks up dust. The water inside the tornado mixes with the dust and makes the tornado look dark. People often say that when a tornado approaches, it sounds like a roaring train.

The U.S. has approximately 700 tornadoes every year; most happen in a Midwest region nicknamed "Tornado Alley." States in the alley include Texas, Oklahoma, Kansas, and Nebraska. Because the area has so many tornadoes, storm chasers often visit there. While some storm chasers are scientists and researchers, others are just people who enjoy seeing **intense** weather up close. This activity is not safe, however. It is best to leave the area during a tornado, if possible, to avoid being seriously injured or killed. Tornadoes may be fascinating, but they are indeed among the fiercest forces of nature. ●

QUESTIONS

1. Which of the following would be the best title for this passage?
   A. Dorothy's Journey
   B. Tornado Alley
   C. Birth of the Tornado
   D. Storm Diaries

2. Which of the following best states the author's purpose?
   A. to inform readers about how tornadoes are formed
   B. to show how harmful the weather can be
   C. to describe how Dorothy made it to Oz
   D. to show why people should move to the Midwest

3. As used in the passage, the word *intense* most nearly means
   A. humble.
   B. strong.
   C. calm.
   D. extreme.

4. Which of the following best states the reason for the last paragraph?
   A. to describe the life of storm chasers
   B. to describe the areas that have more tornadoes
   C. to define a tornado
   D. to tell how many tornadoes happen each year

5. According to the passage, how are tornadoes formed?
   A. Tornadoes are formed by hurricane winds.
   B. Tornadoes are formed in Tornado Alley.
   C. Tornadoes form when the air picks up dust and water.
   D. Tornadoes form when warm air rises and forms a funnel.

6. Which statement best describes a tornado?
   A. A tornado is a violent, destructive, and dangerous windstorm.
   B. A tornado is a violent windstorm that rarely happens.
   C. A tornado is like a hurricane.
   D. A tornado is the reason Dorothy had her exciting adventure.

DIRECTIONS: *Read the passage and answer the questions that follow it.*

Droughts

A DROUGHT IS CHARACTERIZED by a long period of little or no rainfall, which results in quantities of water insufficient to meet the demands of a region. Droughts occur in two forms: seasonal and contingent. Seasonal droughts are normal annual occurrences in tropical countries in regions of Southeast Asia, Latin America, and Africa. These areas have both a rainy and a dry season each year. Usually, the residents of these regions build dams to hold water during the rainy season. During the dry season, this collected water is used to irrigate crops and water livestock. Contingent droughts happen when rainfall averages drop for long periods of time. Certain areas, like the northeastern part of the U.S., experience these droughts frequently, but the cause of reduced rainfall remains unknown.

The word "drought" has three different categorical meanings: meteorological, agricultural, and hydrological. Meteorological drought refers to low levels of rainfall. When most people use the word "drought," they are speaking about this type. Agricultural drought refers to an insufficient supply of water for crops. This can happen even when average rainfall occurs because some soil conditions or farming techniques require more water than others. Hydrological drought happens when the water levels in reservoirs and natural bodies of water fall below average.

Droughts can cause environmental, economic, and social problems. Without rain, crops can wither, and livestock can die from dehydration. Without water and food, people starve or have to move to new areas. This can, and has, led to wars and other social problems. After long periods, the land becomes so dry that dust storms form and wildfires spread over the area. One of the most **devastating** droughts for the U.S. occurred in the 1930s in the Midwest. During this time, the land was so dry that crops could no longer grow and huge dust storms formed, earning the area the nickname "Dustbowl." ●

QUESTIONS

1. **Which of the following would be the best title for this passage?**
   - **A.** The Dustbowl
   - **B.** Dusty Land
   - **C.** Defining the Drought
   - **D.** Hydrologic Droughts

2. **Which of the following best states the author's purpose?**
   - **A.** to inform the reader about the importance of food and water
   - **B.** to inform the reader about the differences between seasonal and contingent droughts
   - **C.** to show how people use the word "drought" incorrectly
   - **D.** to inform the reader how droughts can affect people's lives

3. **As used in the passage, the word *devastating* most nearly means**
   - **A.** crushing.
   - **B.** exciting.
   - **C.** inconvenient.
   - **D.** irritating.

4. **What is the purpose of the second paragraph?**
   - **A.** It describes how people refer to droughts meteorologically.
   - **B.** It discusses the different aspects of drought.
   - **C.** It shows how droughts affect only farmers' crops and livestock.
   - **D.** It shows how droughts are only important to historians.

5. **What is the purpose of the last paragraph?**
   - **A.** It describes where droughts happen.
   - **B.** It shows how little droughts affect human lives.
   - **C.** It shows how much damage droughts can do.
   - **D.** It discusses the historical importance of "Dustbowl."

6. **According to the passage, why does a contingent drought happen?**
   - **A.** Rainfall is higher one year, low the next.
   - **B.** People do not store up adequate water for crops.
   - **C.** Contingent droughts do not happen today.
   - **D.** No one knows why contingent droughts happen.

DIRECTIONS: *Read the passage and answer the questions that follow it.*

The New Winter Sport

SNOWBOARDING IS A relatively new winter sport. Invented approximately forty years ago, it combines the skills and equipment of surfing and skateboarding but is practiced on ski slopes. Skiers and snowboarders often **clash** because some think snowboarding is a less technical sport than skiing, while others think skiing is not as fun and exciting. Snowboarders wear boots strapped horizontally to a wide, wooden board, similar to a skateboard, which they ride downhill through the snow.

While most snowboarders ride on ski slopes, there are four styles of snowboarding: freeride, freestyle, alpine, and backcountry. Freeriders are like surfers in that they ride whatever conditions the mountains offer. They do not focus on tricks or racing. Freestylers practice tricks with their boards on the ground and in the air. This type of snowboarding is influenced by skateboarding and is the most popular style of the sport.

Snowboarding became an Olympic sport in 1998. In the Olympics, men and women compete separately in three categories: halfpipe, parallel giant slalom, and snowboard cross. In the halfpipe competition, snowboarders ride on a U-shaped structure. The athletes ride the pipe to gather speed and then perform acrobatic twists and flips in the air. In the slalom, two snowboarders race each other through tracks. The racer with the quickest speed wins. The snowboard cross is the newest event. In this competition, four snowboarders race one another through an obstacle course. Judges watch the snowboarders and rate their tricks based on the difficulty of the moves, how high they jump, and how they perform overall. The snowboarder with the highest score wins. From its humble beginnings, snowboarding has gained immense popularity as the new exciting, challenging winter sport.●

QUESTIONS

1. The author thinks that snowboarding is

    A. a sport that requires little skill.

    B. much more fascinating than surfing.

    C. a tough but exciting sport.

    D. a sport that needs more press coverage.

2. Which of the following best states the author's purpose?

    A. to explain the rivalry between skiers and snowboarders

    B. to explain the sport of snowboarding

    C. to show how recreational snowboarding differs from competitive snowboarding

    D. to show how snowboarding is not an original sport

3. As used in the passage, the word *clash* most nearly means

    A. battle.

    B. agree.

    C. crash.

    D. discuss.

4. Which of the following statements best describes the reason for the last paragraph?

    A. It explains how men and women compete separately.

    B. It gives the date when snowboarding became an Olympic sport.

    C. It shows differences among the athletes.

    D. It describes how snowboarders compete in the Olympics.

5. What is snowboarding?

    A. Snowboarding is a winter sport that combines surfing and skateboarding.

    B. Snowboarding is a winter sport that uses a vertical board to scale mountains.

    C. Snowboarding is an Olympic sport with one racing category.

    D. Snowboarding is an old sport that has its own unique origins.

6. According to the passage, which statement is true?

    A. Skiers and snowboarders get along on the slopes.

    B. There are three categories of competition in Olympic snowboarding.

    C. Snowboarding is a new spring sport.

    D. Freestyle snowboarding is like surfing.

DIRECTIONS: *Read the passage and answer the questions that follow it.*

Henri de Toulouse-Lautrec

Henri de Toulouse-Lautrec (1864-1901) was a famous French painter. Unlike many artists of his era, he came from a wealthy family and did not have to rely on his art to make a living. This freedom allowed him to paint whatever he wanted. Fascinated by the world of night-clubs, cafes, and dance halls in Paris, he enjoyed observing and sketching the dramatic lives of these people. Toulouse-Lautrec also created many advertising posters about the people he found interesting. He captured

the **atmosphere** and drama that surrounded him by using simple lines and flat colors. Because his images could stir great feeling, posters soon became a new art form.

Although Toulouse-Lautrec was a talented artist who created over 1,000 paintings, 5,000 drawings, and 350 posters, his life was not easy. Before the age of fifteen, Henri had broken both of his femurs in two separate accidents. Henri's legs never healed properly, possibly owing to a genetic defect, and they stopped growing, which left him deformed. His normal torso sat atop his unusually short, underdeveloped legs. Toulouse-Lautrec sometimes perceived that people were laughing at his misproportioned body, and he felt the disability prevented him from fitting in with those of his aristocratic class, so he turned to the cabaret scene of Montmartre in Paris. His desire to belong and his intuitive art allowed him to develop a great sympathy for the lives and struggles of others. Settling into the nightclub scene, however, Henri Toulouse-Lautrec became an alcoholic and died from a mental and physical collapse when he was only thirty-seven. He is now one of the world's most popular artists, and his works are on exhibit in almost every major museum in France and the United States. ◗

QUESTIONS

1. **Which of the following would be the best title for this passage?**
   A. Life of a Solitary Artist
   B. Making Posters Popular
   C. Henri's Adventures
   D. French Art in the 1900s

2. **Which of the following best states the author's purpose?**
   A. to show how people with disabilities are never successful
   B. to explain how advertising posters became popular
   C. to discuss the life of a famous French painter
   D. to show how alcoholism destroys lives

3. **As used in the passage, the word *atmosphere* most nearly means**
   A. air.
   B. people.
   C. area.
   D. environment.

4. **Which of the following statements best describes the reason for the second paragraph?**
   A. It tells how Toulouse-Lautrec died.
   B. It describes his childhood and the reasons why Lautrec returned home to his parents.
   C. It describes why his success was not enough to make him feel as if he fit in.
   D. It describes the impact of his artwork and the reasons for its success.

5. **What effect did Henri's disability have on his life?**
   A. Henri was not affected by his crippled legs.
   B. Henri was able to portray performers' lives realistically.
   C. Henri's disability prevented him from becoming a famous artist.
   D. Henri's disability kept him from going to public places.

6. *Answer the following question using complete sentences:*
   Why might Toulouse-Lautrec have painted subjects from such dramatic walks of life?

DIRECTIONS: *Read the passage and answer the questions that follow it.*

Hurricane:
The Cyclonic Storm

A HURRICANE IS A powerful tropical storm with strong winds, high waves, and heavy rains. In various parts of the world, hurricanes have different names: around the Pacific Ocean, they are called **typhoons**; and around the Indian Ocean, they are called cyclones. The powerful winds and the heavy rainfalls of hurricanes often cause destruction when the immense storms reach land. Winds can destroy lives and property; heavy rains can generate floods. A hurricane's strength is measured by its intensity, which is determined by the wind speed. The Saffir-Simpson scale rates the severity from category one to five, with five being the strongest. Because hurricanes can be so deadly and destructive, warnings are now issued within twenty-four to thirty-six hours of the storm's arrival in a coastal area.

Hurricanes form in areas near the equator where the air is warm and moist. Thunderstorms and tropical depressions (areas of low pressure) help start the formation of hurricanes. The moisture in the extremely humid air around these storms condenses into rain and gives off heat. This heat warms the air and begins to rise. As the warm air rises, it begins to spin and form tight curls. (In the Northern Hemisphere, the air spins counterclockwise; in the Southern Hemisphere, the air spins clockwise.) This mass of whirling air can grow for several days. As it grows, it can range from about 20 to 1,000 miles in **diameter**. The curls form a circle around the center of the hurricane, which is called the eye. In the eye, the weather is calm. Around the eye, however, heavy rains and high clouds form. As the storm grows and strengthens, the air begins to move forward at speeds around ten miles an hour. When the storm moves away from the equator, it speeds up to thirty or forty miles an hour. The winds within a hurricane can range between 74 and 200 miles per hour, but as the hurricane comes closer to land, it becomes weaker because it moves away from its energy source: the warm water. Then, land and wind cause friction, and this slows down and breaks apart the hurricane. Even when this happens, however, it is important to remember that the remaining winds and rains are still extremely powerful and destructive forces of nature. ●

QUESTIONS

1. **Which of the following is not a risk associated with a hurricane?**
   A. property damage
   B. freezing winds
   C. flooding
   D. death

2. **Which of the following best states the author's purpose?**
   A. to show how the Northern and Southern Hemispheres have different weather patterns
   B. to explain how hurricanes are ocean storms that do not reach land
   C. to show how hurricanes form and break down
   D. to explain why people fear tropical storms

3. **As used in the passage, the word *diameter* most nearly means**
   A. width.
   B. height.
   C. length.
   D. average.

4. **Which of the following statements best describes the reason for the last paragraph?**
   A. It describes the eye of a hurricane.
   B. It describes how fast a hurricane moves toward the land.
   C. It describes how a hurricane's strength is measured.
   D. It describes how hurricanes form, move, and disappear.

5. **How are hurricanes measured?**
   A. Hurricanes are measured by how strong the wind speeds are.
   B. A hurricane is measured by the width of its eye.
   C. Hurricanes are measured by the amount of damage they do.
   D. Hurricanes are measured by the amount of rainfall they produce.

6. **What is the difference between Northern and Southern Hemisphere hurricanes?**
   A. There is no difference.
   B. They only have different names.
   C. They produce different amounts of rainfall.
   D. They spin in different directions.

DIRECTIONS: *Read the passage and answer the questions that follow it.*

Comets

IMAGINE LOOKING INTO the sky and seeing a large fire-like object sailing quickly overhead. As it approaches the sun, it becomes brighter and grows a tail. Once it reaches the closest point to the sun, it dims, and the tail disappears. You may soon realize that this bright thing in the sky is a comet. Comets are **celestial** bodies that travel around the sun in orbits, or elliptical paths, around the sun. When a comet's orbit is small, it can be seen every few years with a telescope. Often these comets are hard to see with the naked eye because they are not very bright. Bright comets have larger orbits, which are sometimes completed over the course of thousands of years. These bright comets have distinct tails and can be seen from Earth for a few weeks at a time.

The bright ball of the comet is called the nucleus. It is made mostly of rock, dust, water ice, and frozen gases.

The tail forms as the comet nears the sun. This happens because the ice in the nucleus turns to vapor from the heat. At this time, some of the dust particles are also released.

People have been watching comets for centuries. Aristotle, a famous ancient Greek philosopher, gave the comet its name. He saw similarities between the comet and its tail and the long hair on a person's head. His word for comet, or "kom," literally means "hair of the head." While this was the first word anyone used to discuss a comet academically, the word changed slightly with the passage of time and influences from other languages. Now referred to as comets, these masses of gas, ice, and dust continue to captivate astronomers and other scientists and provide significant clues about the history of our solar system. ●

QUESTIONS

1. Which of the following would be the best title for this passage?

  A. Aristotle's Comet

  B. Dodging Comets

  C. The Comet: A Celestial Body

  D. Naming Space Objects

2. As used in the passage, the word *celestial* most nearly means

  A. heavenly.

  B. earthly.

  C. ugly.

  D. supernatural.

3. Which of the following statements best describes the reason for the last paragraph?

  A. to describe how brilliant Aristotle was

  B. to show how people do not care about comets

  C. to show how the comet got its name

  D. to define the word "philosopher"

4. According to the passage, how is the comet's tail formed?

  A. The tail is formed after the comet passes the sun and the nucleus disappears.

  B. The tail is formed when the sun's heat turns the ice in the nucleus into vapor.

  C. The tail is formed when stars attach to the nucleus during orbit.

  D. The tail is formed after pieces of the nucleus are destroyed by other celestial bodies.

5. Which of the following best states the author's purpose?

  A. to show how objects orbit the sun

  B. to tell how the comet got its name

  C. to describe how comets differ from meteors

  D. to explain the characteristics of a comet

6. According to the passage, which of the following statements is true?

  A. Brighter comets take longer to orbit the sun.

  B. Comets with shorter orbits do not have tails.

  C. People have recently begun to observe comets with telescopes.

  D. Comets are made of dust and particles from other celestial bodies.

DIRECTIONS: *Read the passage and answer the questions that follow it.*

Rodeos

A RODEO IS A CONTEST in which cowboys and cowgirls compete to rope cattle and ride untamed horses (called broncos) and bulls. The word for rodeo comes from the Spanish word for roundup. Rodeo competition began over 100 years ago in the southwestern part of the United States, where many people owned cattle. Cowhands invented racing and roping contests for fun. This idea quickly spread to many towns in the West. Today, this dangerous sport takes place in the U.S., Canada, and Australia.

Rodeos are held in arenas. At one end, there are wooden passageways, called chutes. In riding events, a competitor climbs onto a bull or bronco while it is in the chute. When the rider is ready, the chute is opened, and the animal leaps out wildly. The cowboy's or cowgirl's goal is to stay on the animal for a specific period of time. In saddle bronc riding, the competitor must ride the horse for at least ten seconds. A bucking, leaping horse tries to throw off its rider, who holds on with only one hand and spurs the animal, using spiked metal discs attached to the heel of the boot to dig into the horse and make it move faster. In bareback bronc riding, the rider must ride for eight seconds. In this event, the rider does not use a saddle and must use one hand to hold a belt secured around the horse's middle while using spurs to instigate the horse. In bull riding, the competitor rides a wild bull in the same manner as bareback bronc riding. If a rider falls off the bull, he or she could be crushed by the hooves or **gored** with the horns. Such injuries have killed riders, which indicates what a dangerous sport this really is. Like most professional sports players, these competitors can make a lot of money. Perhaps this is why they put themselves at such risk. ❍

QUESTIONS

1. Which of the following would be the best title for this passage?

    A. Bucking Broncos

    B. How the West Was Won

    C. Cowhands

    D. Dangerous Sports

2. Which of the following best states the author's purpose?

    A. to show how cowboys and cowgirls lived 100 years ago

    B. to describe the different riding events in a rodeo

    C. to get people angry about the mistreatment of cattle

    D. to show how the rodeo got its name

3. Which of the following statements best describes the reason for the last paragraph?

    A. It explains how the riders compete in roping games.

    B. It explains how dangerous bull riding can be.

    C. It explains the rules and risks of competing in rodeos.

    D. It explains how rodeos were invented.

4. Which words might best describe these competitors?

    A. brave, foolish, weak

    B. strong, cowardly, foolish

    C. quick, cowardly, strong

    D. quick, brave, strong

5. As used in the passage, the word *gored* most nearly means

    A. stabbed.

    B. grazed.

    C. pricked.

    D. thrown.

6. Which of the following statements about rodeos is true?

    A. The Spanish invented the rodeo over 100 years ago.

    B. Cowboys must ride broncs and bulls longer than cowgirls do.

    C. Competitors use a saddle and spurs in bareback bronc riding.

    D. Bull riding is the most dangerous riding event.

DIRECTIONS: *Read the passage and answer the questions that follow it.*

Creating the Constitution

We, the people of the United States, in Order to form a more perfect Union, establish Justice, insure domestic Tranquility, provide for the common defense, promote the general Welfare, and secure the Blessings of Liberty to ourselves and our Posterity, do ordain and establish this Constitution for the United States of America.

THE EXCERPT ABOVE is called the Preamble, or the first lines of the Constitution, which explains the basic beliefs of the United States of America. This document defines the Federal Government and places its duties in three branches: the Congress, which has the responsibility of making laws; the President, who has the power to "preserve, protect, and defend" the Constitution; and the Supreme Court, which enforces the laws passed by Congress. America's founders (Thomas Jefferson, Benjamin Franklin, and George Washington, for example) created the different branches so the government would not have absolute power as a king does. They also established basic freedoms for citizens, such as the freedoms of speech and the press, to protect citizens from the government. These basic freedoms are explained in the first ten constitutional amendments, called the Bill of Rights.

Before the U.S. became a unified nation of states, it was a group of thirteen colonies seeking freedom from British rule. Independence was won with the conclusion of the Revolutionary War in 1781. Political leaders soon realized they needed to write a formal constitution that would protect the people. Delegates from the thirteen colonies met at Independence Hall in Philadelphia to begin writing and debating. The fifty-five delegates were divided into two groups: nationalists and states'-righters. The nationalists wanted a strong government, but the state's-righters wanted more power for individual states. To make both groups happy, delegates created the Senate and the House of Representatives. Together, the assemblies make up the U.S. Congress. Once the Constitution was written and Congress was created, the delegates **ratified** the Constitution on September 17, 1787. ●

QUESTIONS

1. **Which of the following statements about the Constitution is false?**
   - **A.** Delegates from the thirteen colonies met in Washington, D.C., to write the Constitution.
   - **B.** The Constitution stands for the basic beliefs of the United States of America.
   - **C.** The first ten amendments are called the Bill of Rights.
   - **D.** The Constitution was ratified in 1787.

2. **Which of the following best states the author's purpose?**
   - **A.** to show how old documents have no meaning today
   - **B.** to show how the different branches of government were formed
   - **C.** to describe the difference between nationalists and states'-righters
   - **D.** to explain why the Constitution was written and what it means for citizens

3. **Which of the following statements best describes the reason for the paragraph following the Preamble?**
   - **A.** It tells who the founding fathers were and why they were important.
   - **B.** It explains the Bill of Rights.
   - **C.** It shows how the U.S. government rules like Britain.
   - **D.** It explains why the three branches were created.

4. **As used in the passage, the word *ratified* most nearly means**
   - **A.** rejected.
   - **B.** approved.
   - **C.** appealed.
   - **D.** debated.

5. **According to the passage, which statement about the Supreme Court is true?**
   - **A.** The Supreme Court makes the laws.
   - **B.** The President is the head of the Supreme Court.
   - **C.** The Supreme Court enforces the laws that Congress passes.
   - **D.** The Supreme Court is the most powerful branch of the government.

6. *Answer the following question using complete sentences:*
   What do the first lines of the Constitution mean?

DIRECTIONS: *Read the passage and answer the questions that follow it.*

The Empire State Building

IN THE MOVIE *King Kong,* a giant ape climbs to the top of the Empire State Building to escape capture, only to fall 102 stories to his death. The scriptwriter chose the Empire State Building for a good reason, perhaps because it is famous for its height. In fact, it was the world's tallest skyscraper for forty-one years. [Only the Sears Tower in Chicago, Taipei 101, and a few others are taller.] The Empire State Building stands at 1,250 feet, or 102 stories, and is New York's tallest building.

A broadcast antenna, which almost all New York's television and radio media now use for **transmissions**, was added to the top of the building in 1952. This addition brought the building's height to 1,472 feet.

The building's construction began on March 17, 1930, led by architects Shreve, Lamb, and Harmon. They designed the building in the then-popular Art Deco style. The construction took a little over one year and forty-one million dollars to complete. Workers finished the building quickly to capture the title of "world's tallest building" from the Chrysler Building in New York City. President Herbert Hoover opened the building on May 1, 1931, by turning on the skyscraper's lights for the first time. Even though the building had been opened officially, most of the office space was not rented until the 1940s. Because of this, the building was nicknamed the "Empty State Building." Now, the building holds over 10,000 office workers.

Workers are not the only people who go to the Empire State Building. Rising on the corner of Fifth Avenue and 34th Street, this famous skyscraper is a popular tourist spot. Fast elevators take people to the top of the building every day of the year. At the top of the observatory, people can see awesome views of New York City. At night, floodlights illuminate the top of the building. The colors of the lights change accordingly to celebrate holidays and national events. Surely because of its many uses, the Empire State Building will continue to be a popular landmark for years to come.●

QUESTIONS

1. **Which of the following would be the best title for this passage?**
    A. Death of King Kong
    B. Empty State Building
    C. NYC Tourist Traps
    D. NYC's Tallest Building

2. **Which of the following best states the author's purpose?**
    A. to discuss the popularity of the Art Deco style in the 1930s
    B. to show how useless skyscrapers can be
    C. to inform the reader about the Empire State Building
    D. to convince more people to visit New York City

3. **Which of the following statements best describes the reason for the first paragraph?**
    A. It explains how tall the Empire State Building is.
    B. It shows how cruel people can be to animals.
    C. It explains why the television and radio media use the building.
    D. It explains how the building lost its title.

4. **As used in the passage, the word *transmissions* most nearly means**
    A. having meetings.
    B. sending information.
    C. watching people.
    D. taking notes.

5. **According to the passage, why was the Empire State Building constructed so quickly?**
    A. to take the title of "world's tallest building"
    B. to end a contest between New York City and Chicago for the world's tallest skyscraper
    C. to be finished before the end of President Herbert Hoover's term
    D. to be used for television and radio broadcasters.

6. **According to the passage, what is the Empire State Building used for?**
    A. The Empire State Building is used for films.
    B. The Empire State Building is just a tourist attraction.
    C. The Empire State Building is used for ceremonies that recognize the President.
    D. The Empire State Building is used by the media, office workers, and tourists.

DIRECTIONS: *Read the passage and answer the questions that follow it.*

Nonviolence Works

MANY PEOPLE OF INDIA consider Mohandas K. Gandhi to be the father of their nation. He has often been called the Mahatma, which means "Great Soul." While he never held political office, he is considered one of the world's greatest figures.

Gandhi was born in western India in 1869, to a family that practiced the Hindu religion. At the age of thirteen, Gandhi married Kasturbai Makanji through an arranged marriage. (In this custom, parents choose a life partner for their child at an early age. The bride and groom sometimes do not meet until the wedding.) Gandhi's family sent him to London to study law. He later spent twenty-one years in South Africa working for Indian rights. While he was there, he led protests and was imprisoned many times. In total, he spent seven years in jail for holding true to his beliefs.

Gandhi returned to India with his wife and children. He soon began helping his people win independence from Britain. As a firm believer in peace, brotherhood, and religious tolerance, Gandhi used nonviolent methods to fight for these beliefs. When religious groups committed acts of violence against the British or each other, Gandhi would fast until the fighting stopped. At one point, he almost died from fasting too long. He has said that "Nonviolence is the greatest force at the disposal of mankind. It is mightier than the mightiest weapon of destruction devised by the **ingenuity** of man."

Gandhi was attending a prayer meeting on January 30, 1948, when, tragically, he was assassinated by a man who disagreed with his political opinions. ●

QUESTIONS

1. **Which of the following best states the author's purpose?**
   A. to inform the reader about Gandhi's criminal record
   B. to explain the political unrest in India
   C. to emphasize the power of nonviolent methods
   D. to show how arranged marriages can work

2. **What is the author's attitude toward Mohandas K. Gandhi?**
   A. The author sympathizes with Gandhi.
   B. The author dislikes Gandhi.
   C. The author strongly disagrees with Gandhi.
   D. The author admires Gandhi.

3. **As used in the passage, the word *ingenuity* most nearly means**
   A. imagination.
   B. stupidity.
   C. hostility.
   D. power.

4. **Which of the following best describes the reason for the second paragraph?**
   A. It explains the cultural practice of arranged marriage.
   B. It gives the details of Gandhi's personal life and early career.
   C. It shows how Gandhi was a criminal who spent time in jail.
   D. It tells how Gandhi got his nickname from the people.

5. **What is the main idea of the third paragraph?**
   A. It shows how Gandhi abandoned his wife and children.
   B. It shows how nonviolent methods never change society.
   C. It details Gandhi's military experience.
   D. It shows how Gandhi fought for India's independence.

6. **What kind of man was Gandhi?**
   A. Gandhi was a firm believer in social justice.
   B. Gandhi was a violent man.
   C. Gandhi traveled the world seeking peace for all racial groups.
   D. Gandhi was raised by Hindu parents, but he never practiced their customs.